Athlete Mental Health Playbook

A beginner's guide to mental wellness for athletes because you're human, not a robot.

Misty Buck

Copyright © 2020 Misty Buck

All rights reserved. No part of this book may be used or reproduced in any manner whatsoever without written permission except in the case of brief quotations embodied in critical articles or reviews.

ISBN: 9781675541357 (paperback)

DEDICATION

To my family: Thanks for sticking by my side and allowing me to know what love means.
To my anxiety: This one's for you, my teacher.

CONTENTS

How To Use This Playbook — vii

Chapter One	Introduction	1
Chapter Two	Life Beyond Performance	5
Chapter Three	What is Mental Health?	8
Chapter Four	Do Only Weak Athletes Have Mental Health Issues?	13
Chapter Five	Bridging the Gap Between Mental Toughness and Mental Health	15
Chapter Six	How Does Mental Health Affect Your Body?	18
Chapter Seven	Play #1 – Building Self-Awareness	22
Chapter Eight	Play #2 – Emotional Intelligence in Sports	24
Chapter Nine	Play #3 – Clearing Your Mental Space	29
Chapter Ten	Play #4 – 10 Super Powered Mindset Shifts	31
Chapter Eleven	Play #5 – Balancing Sports & Life	54
Chapter Twelve	Play #6 – Mindfulness & Meditation	58
Chapter Thirteen	Play #7 – Social Media Strategy	63
Chapter Fourteen	Play #8 – Mental Wellness Worksheets	67
Chapter Fifteen	Play #9 – How to Support Someone Going Through Mental Health Issues	77
Chapter Sixteen	Play #10 – Team Mental Wellness Evaluation	79
Chapter Seventeen	The Final Buzzer	81

About the Author — 83
References — 85

HOW TO USE THIS PLAYBOOK

Disclaimer: The author is not a licensed mental health professional. The content is not intended to be a substitute for professional medical advice, diagnosis, or treatment.

The Mental Health Playbook for Athletes is a beginner's guide to mental wellbeing for athletes, coaches, and teams. The first chapters address common questions about mental health and wellness. The chapters that follow are "plays" to help athletes with mental wellbeing as well as additional "plays" for individuals who support athletes. The interactive Playbook also includes worksheets and exercises.

The content included in this Playbook is intended to provide tools that complement what you're working on with a mental health coach and/or a licensed mental health professional (i.e., psychologist or psychiatrist). As stated in the disclaimer, it is not intended to be a substitute for professional medical advice, diagnosis, or treatment.

CHAPTER ONE

INTRODUCTION

When I first set out to teach athletes about mental health, I did so because I noticed that this population, in particular, had unspoken rules about mental toughness and emotions that needed to be addressed. I grew up around sports and athletes. As the coach's daughter and the sister of an athlete, I was often in the middle of the action on the sidelines during practices and games. I was also a cheerleader, and later a cheerleader coach. I bring this up because this is where I learned to love sports, but it's also where I learned to be tough, walk it off, and never show "weak" or "soft" emotions.

Then, when I was a teenager, I began to experience depression and anxiety. My mental health felt like an ongoing whirlwind of conflicting thoughts and emotions. I didn't feel strong on the inside, but I knew I was supposed to act strong on the outside. I had no idea what was going on with me, or how to make it stop, but deep within my soul, I had a drive to heal and be healed. As I would come to learn, I wasn't the only one struggling who felt like they couldn't show it or talk about it. It took me many years to learn that I'm not crazy or weak and that managing mental wellness truly takes an ongoing mind, body, and soul holistic plan, which is why I'm so passionate about sharing that now.

The purpose of this book is to serve as a beginner's resource for guiding athletes, teams, coaches, and family members to understand and apply mental wellness practices. My goal is to open a dialogue about everyday mental health and provide a holistic perspective of why mental wellness is imperative to overall health and to the enjoyment of life itself. As we go through the Playbook, I'll also share tools that I have found to be helpful.

It should be reiterated that I'm not a licensed mental health professional, but rather someone who has lived through her own mental health issues and who now seeks to help others through sharing my experiences as well as tools that I've learned personally and as a Certified Life Coach.

Rings, trophies, and memories fade. Athletes still have a life to live after all is said and done in their down time, during the offseason, and eventually in retirement.

In looking at the big picture, the one in which we know sports are temporary, the real work in life is achieving a daily well-rounded balance because when we get down to it, everyone's goal is to achieve peace, clarity and happiness. However, when your mental health is off-balance, everything else doesn't seem as important. With that, let's get started.

Mental Health Applies to Everyone

If you're struggling with mental health, you're not alone. According to the National Alliance on Mental Illness (NAMI)[1], approximately 1 in 5 adults in the U.S. (46.6 million) experiences mental illness in a given year. However, many more people deal with issues that can throw their mental health off balance and cause extreme stress. This includes athletes—individuals who are expected to be mentally tough and resilient no matter what.

While the mental health stigma is still a real thing, it's progressively evolving into a conversation that's more acceptable to have as more and more people open up about their struggles. However, with athletes in particular, many find it difficult to admit their internal struggles to themselves, much less to anyone else.

Myth: Athletes are emotionless.

Fact: Athletes are humans, not robots.

Athletes are supposed to be tough and fearless. The "no mercy, win-at-all-costs" culture comes with a price. Anything that extreme is unbalanced. Growing up around athletes, I observed that you weren't supposed to be sad or overwhelmed, at least not for more than a few minutes, but you were supposed to shake it off and be tough. Being sad meant you weren't competing with ruthlessness and no one had time for that. If you cried, you were a "cry baby." That's all there was to it.

Personally, that philosophy didn't exactly work for me, but it did help me. Allow me a moment to explain. It didn't work because I did struggle with mental health no matter how hard I tried to brush it off, but it did help because even in my darkest moments, I was able to reach deep down into my competitive spirit and not give up. My biggest win has been finding ways to care for myself, accept myself, and manage challenges like anxiety while pursuing all that I want in life. It really boils down to having the discipline to stick to my personalized mind, body, and soul routine as well as having the humility to admit when I need more help and the courage to seek it.

I'm not happy because of these things, I'm happy because I found peace within myself, which allows me to enjoy my achievements and manage the flow of life, good or bad.

What I've learned, too, is that pain and hard times are inevitable, but I don't have to suffer. If I can work to overcome my personal problems and find a way to navigate day-to-day stuff that comes up and still be able to achieve happiness, peace, and balance, I know others can too.

As a mental health coach, my goal is to teach athletes to understand and care for their mental and emotional wellbeing. The root of my passion is simple: When I was struggling I needed someone who understood me, accepted me, didn't judge me, and gave me the strength, perspective, hope, and most importantly, the tools to find my inner balance. Mental health is a personal journey. No two journeys look the same, which is why an individualized holistic approach is so important and a major theme throughout this Playbook.

For athletes, sports can be the outlet for everything else going on in his or her life. However, your mental and emotional health can affect your play more than you might realize. For example, long-term stress can be detrimental to your health.

There are many, many studies on the negative effects of stress on the body. That's because stress hormones send your Central Nervous System into a fight or flight response, which is only meant to be a temporary solution in the face of imminent danger. However, chronic stress keeps these hormones flowing. When you hold extreme stress in without addressing it, eventually it's going to find a way out whether that's through breaking your body down, releasing it in bouts of rage, turning to substance abuse, causing a serious issue such as a panic attack, or any other number of outlets. Without managing your mental health, it can easily create bigger problems that seep into all areas of your life.

Imagine all of the problems that you hold inside of you throughout the day, day in and day out. I'm not talking about the things that annoy you here and there; I'm talking about the major stuff that causes you chronic stress. Now, imagine all those things are like popcorn kernels. If you leave those kernels in the heat long enough, they're going to pop and keep popping. That's kind of like what happens when you ignore your problems.

Conversely, I know some of the people reading this are more like me, emotional and sensitive—sometimes referred to as empathic or hyper-sensitive—so it's actually difficult to let things roll off your back without reacting to them. Everything can feel like an attack because you take things personally. I get it; sometimes it's difficult to know what to do with all of your feelings so you either let them all out or maybe you internalize them by beating yourself up. That too can create issues with not being able to think clearly, which in turn may be released through destructive habits that you seek out in order to feel better.

As you'll learn throughout this Playbook, there's an element to balancing reaction and non-reaction to your problems through understanding emotional intelligence, adapting a constructive perspective, non-attachment, and self-development.

When you're not on the court or field, you still have to face the person in the mirror.

CHAPTER TWO

LIFE BEYOND PERFORMANCE

"Everyone loves sausage. No one wants to see how it's made." I first heard this phrase, spoken by Buddy Stephens, during an episode of "Last Chance U." I laughed and it immediately stuck with me because people want to enjoy the end results, but no one wants to think about what it takes to get there. For athletes in particular this rings true because everyone just wants to see them outperform their competitors during a game with incredible athleticism. The crowd loves a flashy show. The average spectator doesn't think about the fact that athletes are human—that is until something goes wrong and even then, the athlete is held to a higher standard because they are considered to be a public figure and, in some ways, superhuman.

> *If we want to protect athletes, we have to serve all of their health needs, not just the ones we can see.*

The pressure of being an athlete, and life in general, can certainly take its toll, which is why it's even more important that we recognize and care for athletes' mental wellbeing. Giving athletes mental health resources and allowing them to voice their issues is critical in an environment that preaches mental and physical toughness.

Life Beyond Performance Truth #1:

Emotions are inevitable but they can also be invisible.

Regardless of what's going on outside of your sport, people expect you to play and perform well. Athletes are taught this as part of the meaning of "mental toughness." Even if you're lucky enough to be a part of an organization that allows you to have space for personal issues, there's likely a threshold for how far that goes. There's a cap space for emotional and mental weaknesses. On top of that, there are the fans that are ruthless in their criticism.

No athlete wants to be seen as weak or lose their spot on the team, so they often brush off their problems and sometimes use it as fuel by channeling their stress into their sport. You can try to force healing all you want; the issues won't go away until you really do the work to heal. Emotions are inevitable yet you can make them seem invisible to others by hiding them as best as you can, but as we'll discuss more throughout this Playbook, eventually that energy is going to go somewhere.

Life Beyond Performance Truth #2:

Physical injury is inevitable.

If you've ever had a physical injury or setback, you know how frustrating it can be. When you're an athlete and this happens, there are other elements that come into play such as frustration from not having the same physical outlet for stress as you're used to and the added question of wondering how well you will or won't recover. Just as emotions are inevitable, so too are injuries.

There are only so many things you can control after an injury. The emotional and mental implications can get into your head and affect your recovery and/or your future play. It can cause anxiety over whether or not you'll ever be the same.

You might wonder things like:

- Will this affect my star rating or my desirability as a draft prospect?
- Will this injury affect my family or the people who count on me for support?
- Will I lose sponsors if I don't start playing again or if I don't play as well as I used to?
- Do I really want to risk long-term damage to my body?
- How do I overcome the mental block of playing scared when I'm nervous about re-injury?

Sometimes, athletes internalize these worries, which can escalate into bigger problems. These seemingly unimportant thoughts, however, deserve attention. Every negative thought habit is another "behind the scenes" factor in not just performance, but in overall mental wellness and the enjoyment of life.

Life Beyond Performance Truth #3:

Life challenges are inevitable.

While it's true that everyone experiences hardships, it's also true that everyone has the ability to cope with them in a healthy manner and eventually, heal. Even when something seems all consuming and insurmountable, in the big picture, the problem and the pain are temporary—that is if you're willing to do the work to work through it. Even when you're deep into a stressful situation, there is a way to manage your stress that is unique to you.

Challenges in life are unavoidable. It is up to you to decide how you want to handle them.

As an athlete, you may feel like you don't have time to focus on anything outside of your sport. Maybe you were taught to give it your all at all costs. Maybe you were also taught that no one cares about your excuses and you need to suck it up. I believe that there is an element of balancing mental toughness and mental wellness, and that it's both possible and necessary to blend the two together. (More on that later.)

Only you can see and feel your life in ways that no one else ever possibly could because outside of the public eye, you're just you. You have to choose what to do with all of the things that you internalize. Although your experience may be unique, it's equally important to understand that you're not weird or broken; you are just living your own experience as a human. You need a plan that works for *you*. You also have to be flexible enough to know that the plan will change, just like in a game, because things happen and you have to be willing to shift your self-care strategy.

Life beyond performance is about understanding that there are innumerable ever-changing situations in each person's life. People think that overcoming physical obstacles are difficult, but I believe that learning to overcome mental wellness obstacles is even more difficult and the reason why many people continue living what I call, "comfortably uncomfortable."

Maybe everyone won't know what it took for you to get to where you are and maybe they will judge you. Whether strangers or family members, each person has their own objective. How committed can you be to staying the course to do what's right for your health regardless of their opinions? Only you know how you feel and only you get to experience your life. You get to choose to persevere mentally, emotionally, spiritually, and physically.

CHAPTER THREE

WHAT IS MENTAL HEALTH?

What is mental health? When people think of mental health, it seems that they generally think of mental illness as if the two were interchangeable. That's a common mistake that I blame on society's stigma. Mental health relates to the wellbeing of one's mental state. Here's a clearer description:

> "Mental health includes our emotional, psychological, and social wellbeing. It affects how we think, feel, and act. It also helps determine how we handle stress, relate to others, and make choices." – MentalHealth.gov[2]

Mental illness, on the other hand, refers to a disorder such as depression, anxiety, Post Traumatic Stress Disorder (PTSD), bipolar disorder, eating disorders, obsessive-compulsive disorders, etc. For the purpose of this Playbook, we'll focus on overall mental wellness.

What can cause mental health issues?

Mental health issues can be linked to a variety of factors. Stress from everyday life can be a catalyst for mental health issues. For example, divorce, death, finances, family tension, illness, school, work, or lack of purpose and direction. The effects of that stress will look different for each person depending on how impactful that incident is and how the person handles emotions (e.g., wearing their emotions on their sleeves or burying their pain, both of which have consequences).

The obvious reason for a mental health issue is a traumatic experience, particularly one that the individual hasn't dealt with or healed from. Other reasons for mental health issues may include emotional imbalance, hormones, genes, dietary deficiencies, physical injury, brain injury, and pretty much anything you can imagine that would impact your brain's function or thought and emotional process.

Mental health looks different on everyone.

It's not uncommon for people to hide trauma out of embarrassment. Emotional trauma can be hidden simply by going unspoken about, but eventually it will manifest into other areas of the individual's life. It's critical, too, that we realize that emotional trauma and our ability to cope with it is different for each and every person.

Everyone deals with things differently due to elements such as personality, upbringing, religion, etc. No two people are the same and no two lives are the same so we all bring different experiences to the lenses through which we view and respond to life. For that very reason, we have to respect when someone has a harder time with a problem than someone else. The mental health process is personal and if we are to trust that process, we have to both acknowledge and respect it.

Mental health issues can also be caused by severe traumatic events or brain damage. Furthermore, issues can arise from a chemical imbalance, which can be triggered by numerous factors.

The point is that mental illness and mental health issues can develop from any number of reasons, which is why it's important to work on mental wellness each and every day and equally important to understand the signs and symptoms of issues. If you're struggling, I highly recommend working with a mental health professional so you can get the right support to help you get back to being you.

Signs of Mental Health Issues

In order to improve mental wellness, we have to understand what issues look like. Sometimes when symptoms are first present, people overlook them because they are unaware of what is causing them or they prefer to ignore them. Some people might even label it as just being in a funk. This misconception is one more reason why everyone should know what to look out for.

Below is a list of some common signs of a mental health issue. Keep in mind that this list is not all-inclusive. Also, if you or someone you know is presenting these signs, it doesn't mean that that they have a serious mental health issue, but it is always worth looking into.

- Loss of interest in activities that used to be fun
- Change in performance in sports, school, or work
- Isolation and withdrawing from social events and friends
- Lack of motivation
- Feeling out of control
- Trouble making decisions or concentrating

- Racing thoughts
- Feelings of hopelessness
- Wanting to sleep all of the time or not being able to sleep at all
- Change in appetite
- Frequent mood swings and outbursts without warning
- Having a hard time getting out of bed in the morning
- Constantly being scared or worried
- Feeling like you can't breathe
- Feeling like you want to take off and run away
- Feeling like you're in a funk
- Poor hygiene
- Always giving but never accepting help nor asking for help
- Overly dependent on one particular thing to make you feel better (i.e., food, alcohol, drugs etc.)
- Not feeling like yourself, even if you can't figure it out why
- Feeling sad but you don't know why
- Knowing you should be sad or angry, but you don't feel anything or you feel numb (i.e. apathetic or emotionally flatlining)
- Feeling extremely stressed when things are out of place or out of order
- Repeated unwanted thoughts or thoughts in a recurring loop
- Afraid that something bad will happen if you don't continuously check on people or things
- Fear of contamination or germs
- Preoccupation with food, eating, weight, etc.

Why mental illness isn't as simple as a choice

Act right. Get over it. Stop feeling sorry for yourself. Toughen up. Everyone has problems so deal with it.

These are just some of the phrases I've heard over the years being told to me or to someone else suffering from a mental health problem.

I believe in tough love. I really do. There's an element in tough love that teaches you to be self-reliant and take responsibility for your own life. But, I also know that mental health problems aren't always as simple as making a choice. There's no "get over it" switch that you can turn on and magically be healed.

People have a habit of assuming that because they cope with stress, emotions, and problems in one way, that everyone else should be able to do the same. False and wildly unfair.

Let's talk for a moment about choices.

- You have the choice to seek help with healing or not. You have the choice to take the steps each and every day to do your best to heal.
- You do not have a 100% choice in the timeframe that it will take for you to heal because mental wellness has layers that are unique to each individual, and they are often invisible. Again, I believe in personal responsibility and the intention/action to heal but there is a delicate balance between will and wounds.
- Mental illness and mental health issues most often don't feel like a choice. Why? The best way to answer this is with one question: Given a choice, who wouldn't want to feel good, pain-free, and at peace?

It doesn't matter what the source of the issue is because the source is an individualized, complicated, unseen abundance of layers and none of us come with a personalized how-to manual.

I adamantly believe that there is a spiritual component to our lives, which means that there are things we all have to go through in order to learn and grow, even when the lesson isn't obvious. It doesn't mean that we are doomed to suffer but it does mean that we will all be faced with challenges and hurdles that again, given another option, we would rather not have to deal with.

For some people, that challenge/hurdle is a mental illness or a mental health issue. And for those individuals, the problem may be temporary or it may be a lifelong battle. Because it can be so complicated, the person may not understand what is going on with them, let alone how to get help.

"Stop being a b----" isn't always the best resolution.

Emotions and negative thinking can't simply be brushed off when they are deeply seeded. You'll notice a theme in this Playbook: your mental and emotional energy always go somewhere no matter how hard you try to bury them. Sometimes the signs of a mental wellness issue aren't clear, but the better you know yourself, the better you'll be able to identify when something isn't right within you. For this reason, one of the first set of "plays" focuses on building self-awareness and emotional intelligence. Both will help you help yourself, but they will also help you with others.

Why is this important? Because in your life as an athlete, you need to be able to hear yourself clearly in order to be able to play clearly. If you want to perform as well as you practice, you have to be willing to practice strengthening yourself beyond your body. You also have to be able to read your teammates and opponents because there isn't time for conversation during competition. And of course, all of this translates into your personal life.

Learn to understand your mental wellness as well as you have learned to understand physical health through practice, training, and respect.

CHAPTER FOUR

DO ONLY WEAK ATHLETES HAVE MENTAL HEALTH ISSUES?

Do only weak athletes have mental health issues? I love this question. An athlete can any have any number of impediments throughout his or her career. We see athletes who come back from serious physical injuries all of the time. We also see athletes with physical disabilities defy the odds and destroy their competition. We don't question the toughness of athletes who overcome physical setbacks; in fact, we praise them for it, so why would we question athletes with mental health struggles?

The easiest answer is that we expect athletes to be mentally tough at all times. But as we've seen with physical injuries, you can overcome a setback and still be considered tough. As another example, what if you have a weakness in your game? Can you focus on improving that? Yes. Additionally, does being tough mean being perfect? No, being tough means getting up when you fall. It means taking a break to fix an injury and training your way back to optimum health.

> *Just as a physical injury can cause excruciating pain, so too can mental health issues.*

Just because it's invisible to another person, doesn't mean it's not there. Sometimes things happen and you can't just get over it or walk it off. Just like you can't simply get over a torn ACL by ignoring it, neither can you just get over a mental health issue by ignoring it.

> *At some point, everyone deals with trauma, stress, sadness, grieving, and a host of other issues that can affect*

your mental health. That doesn't mean you're a weak athlete or weak individual. It means you're human.

Changing the conversation about mental health and wellness begins with perspective. Expecting an athlete to be at peak mental performance 24/7, 365 days/year, is no different than expecting an athlete to be at peak physical performance at all times. Think of a bad day as muscle soreness and a bad week or month as a pulled muscle. Even if you try to ignore it, it's still there. Everyone has emotions and sometimes those emotions don't make us feel great. Everyone goes through hard times. As long as humans have emotions, we'll all have to make mental health a part of our focus and training.

If an athlete is dealing with a mental health issue, that too can be overcome in recovery with therapy and an appropriate care plan decided by a licensed mental health professional. Injury builds character, heart, and strength. It becomes a part of your story, but it doesn't define your story.

What makes an athlete or an individual strong is resilience and the willingness to improve. To improve, you have to admit your weaknesses, no matter if that's physical, mental, or spiritual, and ask for help. That's strength.

CHAPTER FIVE

BRIDGING THE GAP BETWEEN MENTAL TOUGHNESS AND MENTAL HEALTH

Mental health and wellness isn't an issue that is separate from other areas of sports. It's an essential element of the mental toughness that players and coaches seek in their competitive careers. One is tied to the other and it's time we bridge that gap.

Oftentimes athletes equate mental toughness with a hardness that then carries over into all areas of their lives. There has been an entire culture built around the notion that the only feelings that are accepted as "tough" are those of resiliency and aggressiveness. We see many athletes who translate this to mean that if they have something that is emotionally and mentally unhealed, they have to bury it deep within them and keep it there in order to stay competitive. It can also mean that they ignore stress. The implications of these actions can have long-term effects off the field or court and eventually will surface because overcoming emotional and mental adversity is part of being human.

Bridging the gap between mental toughness and mental health in sports

Perspective is everything. Therefore, in order to help athletes understand more about themselves, we have to begin by redefining what mental toughness is.

Mental toughness doesn't mean being emotionless. It's about having the self-discipline to not let your worries or fears get to you.

Tough doesn't mean robotic. It means overcoming adversity by facing it head on. This includes emotions and negative thinking patterns.

Rather than ignoring the issue, confront it conscientiously so that mental toughness and wellness can develop and coexist in the same space. To do this, athletes have to learn to understand emotions (i.e., emotional intelligence) and to develop individualized coping skills.

By widening our definition of mental toughness to include mental training and heightened personal awareness, we begin to open up the space for players to address some of today's most critical issues.

A fear of mistakes is on the rise and it's plaguing mental toughness and mental health.

I've spoken with athletes who say that they are afraid of making mistakes because they feel like they have to be perfect. This is happening at all levels and becoming a widespread fear among players. But, why?

For one, pressure. Athletes feel incredible pressure to exceed and perform as well as develop quicker and at higher levels than ever before. Pressure is all around them mostly because of intense expectations and what the weight of those expectations hold.

An athlete may fear making mistakes for a number of reasons:

- They might feel like their career and their life goals are on the line each and every day
- They may feel like the very livelihood of his or her family is at stake
- They might not want to disappoint people
- They might face vast ridicule (e.g., on social media or in a crowd) and not have the tools to handle that
- They may be overly aware of and insecure about showing weaknesses
- They might have to feel like they have to live up to the idea of who people perceive them to be as an athlete and a person

---

Time Out Strategy Session: Are you willing to make mistakes if it means reaching a goal?

What can be done to help athletes with mental toughness?

There's a way to be mentally tough and resilient while also developing mental wellness as a whole.

It's up to coaches and organizations to make resources available to their players. We can't rely on athletes to develop their mental toughness and wellness when there isn't a culture that encourages the development of mental health. Secondly, we shouldn't assume that an athlete will go outside of his or her sports life to seek mental development. It's imperative to have resources readily available.

A coach can teach physical development, but it can be a lot harder to identify and coach mental development because it's not something that a coach would necessarily physically see. For example, a coach can see a player missing shots or limping, but they can't necessarily see what's going on in his or her head. What if the athlete chooses to hide or ignore his or her internal issues? Then what?

The best way to help athletes is to keep an open forum by talking about the issues they face regularly and making sure they know who to go to and that they feel okay doing so.

What can athletes do to develop mental toughness and mental wellness skills?

Even with the right support, mental toughness and mental wellness is ultimately up to the individual. He or she might be in the best environment with the best resources, and the athlete would still have to be the one to take responsibility for his or her personal development.

Athletes are in an advantageous position because they already understand that it's impossible to control 100% of what happens during competition. This same mentality transfers over to every other area of life. Just like it's up to the player to decide how to react to the flow of the game, it's up to them to develop the skills to effectively play through the flow of life.

This isn't always easy. There are innumerable challenges in personal development because we are forced to face uncomfortable wounds, make tough decisions, to speak our truth, stand behind that truth, admit our faults, and make an effort to change negative habits. Is it possible? Yes. Is it worth it? Yes.

Once an athlete is committed to this improvement, they can try seeking out help from their coaches or look for mental health professionals or coaches to help. But first, we have to accept that mental toughness and mental wellness are not separate issues. Both are integrated into our daily lives.

CHAPTER SIX

HOW DOES MENTAL HEALTH AFFECT YOUR BODY?

"The brain doesn't know the difference between what we think and what we experience. So if we imagine or think about something related to the past or the future, on some level we will experience that event—including all the emotions it provokes." – George Mumford, The Mindful Athlete[3]

If we look at overall health as a balance of mind, body, and soul, it's easy to see how the energy of one affects the others. If one of these is imbalanced, it can throw off the others. For example, a physical injury can derail your mindset; a previous traumatic experience can affect the decisions you make; or if you feel lost in who you are, you can feel unmotivated and tired.

> There are endless ways that mind, body, and soul energy—both physical and metaphysical—work together and react together.

Let's explore stress again as an example because everyone can relate to it. This energy affects your physical energy, your decision-making, and your ability to perform. Stress is both draining and distracting. Not only can it affect your ability to perform on a daily basis, but it can also break down your body or turn into other issues over time. This is because your body is not meant to stay in a fight or flight state for long periods of time. Therefore, not addressing an issue can have detrimental results. For some that might mean anxiety or maybe depression or angry outbursts or self-destructive behavior. Again, it looks different for everyone.

But, I'm fine.

When you're someone who prides yourself on being tough and able to handle anything, stress and its consequences are one of the last things you might think about.

"I'm fine."

How many times have I uttered these words feeling like I was barely holding it together yet strong enough to handle anything, and so I didn't have time to feel. I only had time to keep moving forward.

I went through a period in my life when my body started breaking down. It was then that I realized, maybe I really was stressed and not really as fine as I thought I was. Symptom after symptom and doctor after doctor, all with the same diagnosis, "you're stressed."

*Um, excuse me? **I'm fine.***

As I was driving home from one of these doctor's appointments, a light bulb hit. *Maybe I'm so used to being stressed that it feels normal. I'm so used to feeling like I'm underwater and constantly in survival mode that this feeling is my normal way of living.*

And then, an alarm went off. *My body is breaking down because I'm in a constant fight or flight mode, yet I feel normal.* That thought rocked me with fear.

Emotional, cognitive or physical, there are a variety of ways that your body will try to tell you that you've been under too much stress for too long. When you think you have everything under control, it can be easier to bury and explain away emotions like moodiness and behaviors like sleeplessness, forgetfulness, or an inability to focus.

There could be a million reasons for your symptoms, right? And if you "feel normal," you'll look for any answer possible to fit the reasoning that the problem is out of your control. Stress is one of the last things on your list because you can't possibly be stressed. You got this and you're doing *just fine*. I thought the same thing. It took a wake up call for me to learn the lesson the hard way.

Your mind, body, and emotions will tell you everything you need to know if you're willing to listen. The goal is to avoid emergency situations by helping yourself from the get-go. Everyone needs help here and there. Even those who are self-reliant need assistance here and there in order to become even stronger.

The consequences of long-term stress are a reality. It can exacerbate an underlying minor cognitive, emotional, or physical issue or it can create completely new ones. Emotional stress needs an outlet. You have a choice in that.

Mental wellness is inescapable for every athlete, regardless of his or her level, on and off the field or court.

Even if you're a star athlete and doing things other people can't because of your physical talent and sports IQ, you can only become more competitive in all areas of your life by making an effort to balance your mind, your body, and your soul, which I can assure you not everyone is willing to do.

The strongest competitors train in preparation of both known and unknown physical weaknesses. However, most people aren't willing to look at weak points in their thinking or emotional intelligence. There could be invisible things holding you back because you've learned how to cope with it, you've accepted it as the way that life is, or it has become a part of how you identify yourself.

Every single person has experiences that have shaped who they are and those experiences ultimately help shape their thinking process.

Personality is a natural contributor to a person's perspective, but again, it's personal and individual, which means sometimes we hold on to things that don't serve us without even realizing it.

Here's my theory on that: Experiences become beliefs. Beliefs become thought habits. Thought habits become emotions. Emotions dictate action. All of this is energy.

For example, let's say that you touch a hot stove (the experience). You burn your hand and you learn that it hurts (belief that if you touch a hot stove, you'll get burned). Now you know not to touch a hot stove (this is a thought habit because it's a belief you've accepted as a fact and therefore you never second guess it). When you think of touching a hot stove, you think of pain (a feeling that leads you to take action to never touch another hot stove). This is good if the experience leads to a protection that you need to stay safe and healthy, but think about all of the experiences that have led you to make decisions that hold you back. What about negative things that people have said to you that you then accepted as the truth about who you are?

I use this theory and hot stove example often to illustrate how mental health and wellness is directly related to mental, spiritual and physical energy because even if you feel okay, there's always something to improve upon that can open you up to not only performing better, but to enjoying life more. Fortunately, our brains are super smart and include this thing called neuroplasticity, which simply means that we have the ability to change and rewire it. So, you're not stuck. You have the ability to transform negative thought habits, which is pretty cool. Throughout the rest of this

Playbook, we'll look at different "plays" that can be helpful to your overall mental wellness through a variety of tools including reframing negative thought habits.

Before we get into the "plays", however, here's what I want you to reiterate if you're struggling with mental wellness issues:

1. You're not alone.
2. Things will get better if you're willing to participate in your healing with the same discipline that you approach your sport with. This means that there might be things that you don't really want to do or don't think you need to do, but doing them anyway is part of having the discipline to achieving your goal. If, however, something is way too uncomfortable, as in healing trauma, seek the help of a professional and go at a pace that you are comfortable with.
3. It will probably feel painful and uncomfortable before it feels better, but it's up to you to decide how much healing you want to do and when you want to do it (there's no right or wrong answer to that time period, by the way.)
4. I strongly suggest working with a professional to help you work through this because mental health isn't a 100% DIY project. I don't care how independent you are or how strong you are, everyone needs someone to help them with the right perspective and to set an accountability plan.
5. You'll have days when you feel like you're making progress and days when you feel like you're going backwards. Everyone goes through this. Take time for extra self-care during the harder times. Reach out for additional support. Rest if you have to, but keep going.

IF YOU FEEL LIKE YOU'RE HAVING AN EMERGENCY SITUATION, CALL 911. YOU CAN ALSO CALL CRISIS HELPLINES. THE NATIONAL SUICIDE PREVENTION LIFELINE IS A NATIONAL NETWORK OF LOCAL CRISIS CENTERS THAT PROVIDES FREE AND CONFIDENTIAL EMOTIONAL SUPPORT TO PEOPLE IN SUICIDAL CRISIS OR EMOTIONAL DISTRESS 24 HOURS A DAY, 7 DAYS A WEEK. 1-800-273-8255

CHAPTER SEVEN

PLAY #1 – BUILDING SELF-AWARENESS

Now that we know what mental health and wellness is and why it's so important, it's time to work on some tools or "plays." The first "play" of the Playbook is to learn to understand your thoughts and emotions the way you have learned to understand your body. This is because before we can get into how to improve and manage mental wellness, you need to develop self-awareness.

The very first step is to become aware of your mental health and to check-in with yourself periodically about how you're feeling. It's not lame, by the way, to increase your self-awareness. In fact, the strongest and most successful people I know make that practice a priority. Being in your feelings and being aware of your feelings are two different things. For the purpose of this chapter, I'm speaking of the latter.

Learn to hear yourself and respect what you are feeling.

If you are going through something emotional, give yourself permission to sit with your feelings. Sitting with your feelings doesn't mean that you're wallowing in self-pity or feeling sorry for yourself or overthinking. It means that you're addressing what's going on by giving yourself the space to clear your mind and be real with yourself. For example, let's say a family member passes away, but you don't give yourself time to deal with how that makes you feel, it could later manifest into a much bigger issue. That energy has to go somewhere.

You can't move on if you don't first recognize what's going on.

One of the primary keys in managing your mental health is having the ability to identify the things that cause your emotional reactions. A lot of times there is a pattern to those things, which is what I work with athletes on in coaching and something you can work on with a mental health professional as well. Commonly known as "triggers," these are things that cause you to have a specific emotional response. The reason this is so important is because it helps you choose your reaction before it happens. It's like preparing for any other scenario in a game. I'll give you an example. One of my top pet peeves is when people lie to me so when someone lies to me, I know that I have to pause before I speak so that I maintain in control of my response instead of allowing my emotions to lead the conversation.

There are lots of ways to heighten your self-awareness, and I offer some throughout this Playbook, but for starters, check in with yourself and simply become aware of how you are feeling at any given moment.

Here are a few simple questions you can ask yourself each day:

- How did I feel when I woke up?
- How do I feel now?
- If I were an emoji right now, which one would I be?
- What made me happy today?
- What bothered me today?
- Is there a pattern to the things that set off my negative emotions?

CHAPTER EIGHT

PLAY #2 – EMOTIONAL INTELLIGENCE IN SPORTS

You're human; not a robot, which means you have emotions. Just like you have a sports IQ and other areas of knowledge that you work to develop, you also have what's known as, "emotional intelligence" or EI. This is a critical part of mental wellness, mental toughness, performance, personal development, and so much more. We can't escape that fact that we have emotions; so, learning how to understand them and manage them should be natural. However, we often learn about emotions from experiences and as the last chapter addressed, those lessons aren't always healthy. Emotions are complicated because sometimes they feel uncontrollable and/or they take us by surprise. Improving your emotional intelligence can help you by providing a deeper understanding of yourself, and of others.

What is emotional intelligence?

"Emotional intelligence refers to the ability to identify and manage one's own emotions, as well as the emotions of others. Emotional intelligence is generally said to include at least three skills: emotional awareness, or the ability to identify and name one's own emotions; the ability to harness those emotions and apply them to tasks like thinking and problem solving; and the ability to manage emotions, which includes both regulating one's own emotions when necessary and helping others to do the same." – PsychologyToday.com[4]

Looking at this definition, we see that the three main components of emotional intelligence include identification, application, and management. We unconsciously go through this process all day, every day. What we may not do is take the time to develop these skills. The way someone handles his or her emotions is part personality and part learned behavior although factors such as hormones and brain development can also play a role. What marks the level of emotional intelligence is just like anything else in life; it's what you learn, how you practice, and what you do with it.

What is emotional intelligence in sports?

Emotional intelligence in sports is an extension of the individual's mental toughness and mental wellness capabilities. For instance, we've all seen an athlete explode or implode during a game or afterward in the locker room. We've also seen athletes remain completely cool under pressure. His or her emotions lead those reactions. Understanding those differences is part of emotional intelligence.

When we judge an athlete's emotional maturity or depth, we're essentially talking about his or her emotional intelligence. Here's why that matters in sports: Competition is emotional in nature because as the definition of the word implies, it's a rivalry. Therefore, emotional intelligence in sports is as much a part of the contest as any other factor. However, in practice, it's often understated or even ignored when in reality, training players' emotional intelligence could impact their athletic performance and their life as a whole for the better.

Why is emotional intelligence important in sports?

Have you ever heard someone say, "don't let your emotions get in your way" or conversely, "think from your heart." Emotions are woven into every moment of our lives. We "feel" our way through any given moment and act accordingly. Why do some people have more control over their emotions than others? It's nature and nurture meaning that at the most rudimentary level, it's part personality and part learned behavior.

Somewhere on the scale among hypersensitive, reactive, controlled, or apathetic, an individual's emotions will largely determine their actions because they are making decisions from their emotional state. It's human nature to do so and the reason that people say things like, "emotions cloud judgment." The development of emotional intelligence not only affects the individual on a personal level, but also in their ability to read others. Both of these skills are critical for athletes who seek mental toughness, a clear mind, and the ability to compete more effectively.

As an example, if an athlete is easily angered or rattled, he or she might overreact during their play, lose their clear focus, or let an opponent get in their head, which might derail the rest of the game and in some cases, carry over for longer periods of time. An emotional intelligent athlete, on the other hand, may identify what stirs those negative emotions and learn how to manage them before they disrupt their thinking and decision-making.

Emotional intelligence in mental health

Sports aside, emotional intelligence is a game changer in developing mental wellness. Although there are numerous studies and theories that dive deep into the principle of emotional intelligence, it's really pretty basic. Let's go back to the three fundamental components: identification, application, and management.

When you can identify what your emotions are and where they are coming from, you can then apply different thought habits and tools, which then allows you to manage triggering situations and emotions in healthier ways. Here's what that might mean:

- Rather than feeling like your emotions are out of your control, you can learn to understand them so that when something doesn't feel right, you can say to yourself, "I know where this is coming from." That's a really critical step in moving from accepting those negative feelings as part of who you are (angry, sad, depressed, anxious, insecure, etc.) to understanding that those reactions aren't necessarily coming from you, but rather coming from experiences. (Remember my theory from Chapter Six: Experiences become beliefs. Beliefs become thought habits. Thought habits become emotions. Emotions dictate action.)
- In a moment when you are able to recognize the source of your emotions, you can then recognize, "this emotion is related to this." Now, you have the opportunity to apply a different way of thinking or another coping skill. In other words, the emotion becomes an opportunity because it is a compass that shows you what is going on internally. For example, if you are feeling anxiety, rather than letting it run uncontrollably (as anxiety often feels like), you can at least breathe and understand what's going on, which can provide a level of comfort. You can then use different coping skills and healing tools to help you navigate the situation in the moment and beyond. Additionally, you can learn to understand all of your emotions, not just the negative ones, because again, it's about learning. Which emotions keep you motivated? Which emotions help you compete? Which emotions produce grit to get you through tough times? Which emotions keep you safe in dangerous situations? Which emotions help you receive love and give love?
- While some of this process takes place in the moment, learning to understand and manage your emotions happens all day every day throughout your entire life. Part of it is maturity and part of it is getting to know yourself.

Emotions aren't a bad thing. They tell you what you need to know about so many different areas of your life (mind, body, and soul) so learning to recognize them, understand them, and manage them can make a really big impact in your lifelong quest for peace and happiness.
- The other component to consider is your emotional intelligence of other people's emotions. While you can't make anyone feel anything, you can certainly understand how to perceive the emotions that other people feel. This doesn't mean accepting responsibility for their emotions nor does it mean that you can act however you want and expect people to accept that behavior. It does mean that you can open up to seeing situations from a broader or more objective viewpoint, which will help you to both, not take things personally and also understand situations and people in a healthier way.

Questions to develop your emotional intelligence

An individual's emotional intelligence can be improved by taking the time to become aware of his or her feelings and how those feelings affect their thinking, decision-making, etc. The idea is to deepen your self-awareness so that you begin to understand the things that push your buttons so you can then work on managing those emotions and your reactions.

Below is a series of questions that you can use as an exercise:

1. How did I feel when I woke up this morning? (Think of various aspects of your life. For example: How did my body feel? What emotions did I feel? How did I feel spiritually?)
2. What emotions did I feel throughout the day?
3. What made my emotions change?
4. How did other people impact my emotions?
5. How did my thoughts, words, and actions impact my emotions?
6. What actions did I take because of how I was feeling in the moment?
7. What can I learn from this and what new habits or thinking patterns, if any, can I work on?

The other half of emotional intelligence is learning to understand other's emotions. For an athlete, that might mean gaining a deeper understanding of teammates or even opponents. Here are a few questions to help you begin to understand others while also becoming aware of your responses to them.

1. What does this person appear to be feeling?
2. How is their reaction/action affecting how I respond to them?
3. What would be an emotionally mature response?
4. How can I be supportive and understanding without absorbing their emotions? How can I be supportive and understanding with compassion? (This question is phrased two different ways because one person might be very sensitive and therefore, they might take on the other person's emotions as if it were their own emotions while another person might put up a "wall" and be shut off from how another person is feeling altogether.)

Time Out Strategy Session: Log your emotions for three days. Write down every emotion that you feel. At the end of the day, use the series of questions above to help you understand those emotions. This exercise is not to "fix" anything, but rather to help you being to understand yourself a little bit better.

CHAPTER NINE

PLAY #3 – CLEARING YOUR MENTAL SPACE

Before we can talk about mental health and wellness management, we need to talk about what to do when you are struggling with something. If you're going through a tough time, give yourself permission to feel it and heal it. Be real with yourself about what you're feeling. If something feels off or you feel like you're in a funk, there's a reason for that. As mentioned earlier, mental wellbeing is a personal process so respect your process.

Make time for self-awareness through reflection

In the previous chapter we talked about why self-awareness is important. To do that, it requires that you take time for self-reflection. Healing begins when you give yourself a chance to be clear with yourself on how you're feeling. Clearing your mental space can happen by something as simple as slowing down and chilling out on your own. You don't need a big a-ha moment. You just need to give yourself breathing room away from pressure and distractions.

Learn to say, "no" to the things that don't bring you closer to your goal and "yes" to the things that do in order to invest in yourself.

Below are some things you can do during your self-reflection time. This will work best if you do these activities by yourself. I also strongly suggest that you take a technology break. No texting, emailing, social media, game playing, TV watching, etc. Limit your distractions so you can clear your mind and be with your thoughts. A word of caution: Sometimes being alone with your thoughts can be overwhelming because sometimes mental illness issues mean that your thoughts might be racing, looping, or otherwise unpleasant. If that is the case, work with a mental health professional who can help you through this.

- Write
- Go on a walking meditation
- Go on a run
- Lift weights
- Listen to music in a quiet space
- Sing
- Draw
- Paint
- Sit outside and observe the world
- Clean or organize a room
- Hang out with your pets
- Read a book on the topic of your issue
- Meditate

Time Out Strategy Session: Writing Exercise

Write a letter to the person or thing that's bothering you or write a letter to the emotion that you're feeling. Afterwards, you can burn it, shred it, throw it away, step on it, and destroy it if you want to, but you may be surprised at what transpires. Just write everything that comes to you. Don't stop to go back and read what you wrote before you're finished. Let it flow. Don't judge it. Just write until you feel you've said your peace. If you can't come up with anything to write, try writing about your issue from someone else's perspective.

CHAPTER TEN

PLAY #4 – 10 SUPER POWERED MINDSET SHIFTS

What if I told you that your super power is your mind and that everyone has this power? As an athlete you probably work a lot on vision, toughness, grit, etc., which means that you probably had to train your mindset about certain parts of your game here and there. These same principles can help you improve your mental wellness, but you have to know what to look for. This is why the first "plays" were about the importance of self-awareness, building emotional intelligence, and making time for clarity because the thing is, no one knows what you're thinking and feeling but you. And, sometimes those thoughts and emotions get muddied up and pushed away so that you can focus on doing your job as an athlete. However, once you start recognizing and respecting all of your thoughts and emotions, you can then work to change them.

The thing about mental health issues is that they can often feel disempowering because it can feel hopeless, frightening, and even uncontrollable. This is why mindset shifts can help with getting on the path to peace. If you recall from the previous chapter, your brain has the ability to change throughout your entire life because of something called neuroplasticity, which means you have the ability to rewire negative thought habits into ones that are more positive, productive, and peaceful. The mindset shifts that follow are based on the most common mentality blocks that I encounter in my conversations with athletes.

Mindset Shift #1: Mental Health is a Strength

Changing the stigma of mental health in sports begins with changing the way we think about it. The phrase "mental health" is often coupled with notions of disgrace. The observer may say that the person with a mental wellness issue is weak and begin to look at them as a weak link in a win-at-all-costs culture. The individual who is suffering may feel humiliated for feeling anything other than tough.

What would happen if we simply decided that mental health is a strength and deserves the daily training, attention, and respect that our body does?

We are beginning to see this shift occur in pro sports, specifically the NFL and the NBA, which both developed mental wellness policies to assist their players and personnel. Still, a policy can only do so much, which is why it's imperative that we start thinking of the mind as a part of the whole athlete, not a separate entity.

Furthermore, we must respect our own mental wellness as an individual. Rather than being judgmental of the way we feel, allow the emotions to lead you to what needs healing. Just like a pain in your body, emotions and thoughts deserve your attention. The development of these things can help you become stronger.

Time Out Strategy Session: In your own words, why should mental health be considered a strength instead of a weakness?

Mindset Shift #2: Rest is a Discipline

Taking breaks is so much more important than we often realize. It's so easy to stay in a routine of constantly pushing to get through our routines. Most people I know, including myself, feel guilty for taking breaks because then you feel like you're going to fall behind or let someone down or be called lazy. For others, you might feel like you just flat out don't have the time to take a break. We're taught to be disciplined and tough, but I want to introduce the idea of disciplined rest to complement your disciplined work.

The fittest people on the planet know that your body needs rest and the sturdiest people know that your mind also needs rest.

The concept of mental rest is still something that's evolving as an accepted part of mental health and self care. However, the concept of physical rest is completely accepted when really the needs for mental and physical rest are no different.

First, let's examine physical rest. I'll use weight training as an example because it's what I am most familiar with. If you talk to any athlete, body builder or even just your local gym rat, they'll tell you that if you want results, your body needs rest. When you lift weights and you're sore the next day, it's because the action of lifting weights has caused microscopic tears in your muscles therefore putting them in a state of repair. To help your muscles out during this period of rebuilding and growth, you have to do a few things such as get proper nutrition, hydration, and rest. If you never let your muscles rest, they can't optimally heal and grow. Plus, you're risking injury because your body hasn't had time to repair back to 100%.

To put it another way, not resting your body is like getting an air leak in your car tire and driving around without ever fixing it. Your car won't perform well, it'll take forever to get anywhere, and eventually, you'll make it worse until the car won't move at all.

So, if we understand this about our physical workouts, injuries, and even our cars, why don't we accept rest and repair as a discipline in our mental health and overall health?

Give yourself permission to rest regularly and be disciplined about it. You're not a machine... and even machines break!

Tips to help you take mental health breaks:

- Make your rest enjoyable! Your rest routine should help you relax and loosen up. Plan to do things that you enjoy. You're more likely to keep up with it.
- Stop trying to be prove your worth by killing yourself all day, every day. You're enough. You can chase your goals, push yourself to improve, and still respect the needs of your mind, body, and soul.
- Fear of Missing Out (FOMO) is real, but you should fear missing yourself more.
- Stand up for yourself and claim your breaks. If you feel like you're going to inconvenience someone with your rest, they'll get over it because well, they'll just have to.
- On that note, sometimes breaks happen in the form of a boundary that you create with others. For example, stop letting people take you for a ride on their crazy trains. There's a difference between being supportive and in taking on responsibility for where someone else is in his or her life. Pay attention to the buttons they push so you're better equipped to say, "no."
- Remind yourself that you're the only one who has to live your life and the people who depend on you want you to be at your best and need you to be at your best. That can't happen if you're constantly running on "E." In keeping with the car theme that is emerging here, refuel and cool off your engine. Totally acceptable, my friend!
- Take note of the things you feel burnt out on and exhausted from. There might be a way to reframe some thinking habits around these parts of your life so that you give yourself an emotional break.

Time Out Strategy Session: How can you work in mental breaks into your schedule? When you will you schedule that time? What will you do with that time?

Mindset Shift #3: Self-Talk is a Major Key in Mental Wellness

"Remember, you have been criticizing yourself for years and it hasn't worked. Try approving of yourself and see what happens." – Louise L. Hay

It happens everyday. We have conversations and inner dialogues with ourselves through our thoughts. Sometimes our thoughts are as mundane and routine as, "lock the door before you leave the house" and sometimes they are more complex manifestations of how we feel about ourselves, others, and our world. It's not unusual for some of these thoughts to be so habitual that it's almost as if they are a part of our subconscious and engrained in our daily lives to a degree that we are unaware of them.

Here is one example. From a young age, most of us are taught that self-deprecation is funny. We learn to poke fun at ourselves or to not take ourselves so seriously. For example, if you have a habit of thinking "I'm so stupid," even if you don't really think you're stupid, you're engraining that somewhere into your subconscious and therefore giving yourself permission to take action that matches your belief. It can become an excuse that you hang on to so somewhere down the line it then becomes acceptable for you to then think things like, "of course it didn't work out, I'm not that smart anyway." Sometimes we develop self-criticism because others have told us from a young age that we are dumb, slow, overly sensitive, self-centered, etc. Regardless of why we've adopted these negative beliefs about ourselves, they are a part of who we are until we work to change that.

"The goal doesn't have to be perfection. It can just be peace and acceptance with yourself." – Ben Gordon[5]

Self-criticism is a common block in mental wellness.

Why is it so easy for me to be so kind to other people, yet it's also so easy for me to be so hard on myself? I asked myself this question one day when I was experiencing anxiety that was seemingly "out of the blue." I then thought, *there has to be a better way of self-motivation than self-deprecation.* Interestingly enough, when I researched this, there were several experts who saw this behavior as a way of self-regulating the ego through the act of self-deprecating humility and also as a way to fit into societal norms.

This makes total sense for several reasons. You might have thoughts like:

- If I stop to congratulate myself or enjoy my accomplishments, society says that I'm being self-absorbed.
- If I stop or pause, I'm going to get run over by someone else who is running the same race.
- If I tell myself, that's good, but not good enough, I'll stay motivated.
- It's more acceptable to talk poorly about myself in public than to say, hey, I'm proud of myself.

If we are to go a layer even deeper, I believe that anxiety and anxiety attacks are often (not always) the result of negative thought habits. These thoughts can emerge from thought patterns such as obsessive-compulsive disorder (also known as OCD), insecurities, fears, anticipatory anxiety, etc. In my own life, I have found that the anticipation of bad things happening can be boiled down to a negative thought habit. I'll share another personal example.

One of my anxiety triggers is around finances. I used to be extremely afraid that I'm not going to have enough money and I'm going to lose everything and be completely unstable and unable to support myself. That's quite unlikely, but it's a fear of mine that was deeply rooted, and therefore an entrenched habitual perspective that I applied in my life. I found that this fear is really a fear of having things happen outside of my control that will result in a great loss or instability. Even though I've discovered the reasons for that fear, it still sneaks up on me now and then. Why? It is fairly improbable that years and years of the same negative self-talk would vanish in an instant from one positive thought because at some level, it has been a part of who we think we are. It's something that I have to work at.

There are several sections and exercises that address how to begin to retrain your mindset throughout the remainder of this Playbook, but the overall point here is that your self-talk is ultimately the perspective through which you view life and therefore a major key in your mental wellness. It's a process that takes discipline just like any other training.

Time Out Strategy Session: Over the next week, take note of the negative things that you say about yourself. Write them down here. When the week is over, come back and look at the list and write down your observations.

Mindset Shift #4: Reframe Negative Thoughts with Affirmations

As obvious as this may seem, your mental health has a lot to do with your thoughts. Sometimes it's not as easy as "think good, feel good," especially if you're going through a hard time. However, training your brain with positive affirmations can begin to transform your overall wellness. Being aware of and deliberate with your thoughts is an important first step to any wellness routine.

Most everyone has negative thought habits that they have adapted. Perhaps you've started to notice some as you've gone through this book. Working with affirmations can create a monumental shift in your overall wellbeing by training your mind to focus on what feels good and what you want instead of what's scary or uncertain.

In the worksheets section that follows, there is an entire exercise dedicated to working with affirmations, but as a starting point, I'm sharing some phrases that you can say upon waking up in the morning that can help you set the tone for the day. You can use these at any point during your day as well.

- What's the best that can happen?
- Really good things are happening right now. (Affirm, yes they are.)

- Today is going to be the best day ever. (Affirm, yes it is.)
- I release resistance in order to allow miracles into my life. (Yes, I do.)
- Thank you. Thank you. Thank you.

The universe responds to positivity with positivity, but more importantly when you feel good, you give yourself the opportunity to do better for yourself by lifting yourself up. You also have more, and longer-lasting, physical energy when your mindset is in the right place. If your mindset derails during the course of the day, pause, take a few deep breaths, and repeat your affirmations. You can even write them down several times while you take a break and breathe.

> Time Out Strategy Session: What negative thought habits do you have? Begin to observe them. Is there a pattern? Write your answers below. (We all have negative thought habits by the way; it doesn't mean there is anything wrong with you. However, adopting a more positive mindset can help you feel more peaceful.)

Mindset Shift #5: Celebrate All of the Wins

The importance of gratitude in mental wellness is to open up your mindset to all of the positive possibilities by expanding your viewpoint to see beyond to-do lists, unreached goals, worries, doubts, fears, etc. This is not about being preachy or overly/

blindly optimistic. Gratitude is about appreciating the little things so that you can enjoy every moment while you grow into bigger things. Being an athlete and making the team is a gift in and of itself. I know I don't have to tell you that, but I say it because it's easy to take for granted.

Gratitude, in its simplest meaning, is being thankful for everything you have. If you ever injured something, you'll know what it feels like to wonder how you ever took your health for granted. For example, if you break a finger with your dominant hand, you know what it's like to wish you could do something as simple as write your own name. However, you can still be grateful that you didn't completely lose your finger. See where I'm going with this?

Exceptional athletes are constantly trying to improve, which means they are focusing on their flaws in order to correct them. You can be grateful and still become a better player. Gratitude doesn't mean being so satisfied with the status quo that you don't have to work to improve and be your best. It means knowing you can succeed because wherever you are right now is proof that you can develop and grow from where you were. Google quotes on gratitude and you'll see extremely successful people who make it a point to be grateful.

One simple way to express gratitude is by celebrating small wins. Below is an example of some questions you can ask yourself. Keep in mind this is not a checklist. You don't have to check off the answers to all of the questions in order to equal a win. One question answered equals a win. It's not a contest and there are not right or wrong answers. My hope is that you open up your mindset to looking for things to celebrate with these or other questions.

What wins can you celebrate?

- What did you do right?
- What things are you grateful for in this moment? (I count everything from my head to my toes and beyond.)
- What fills your heart with joy?
- Did you follow your intuition?
- Did you stand up for yourself?
- Did you go through your day instead of giving up?
- Did you give yourself time to rest and recharge?
- Did you push yourself past a comfort zone?
- Who can you count on to talk to?
- What compliments do people give you?
- What did you achieve today?

- What big achievements have you reached in your life?
- Have you been kind to people even when you didn't feel great yourself?
- Did you help someone?
- Did you take time for out yourself even when other people wanted to demand more of your time?
- Did you keep a boundary that you set?
- Did you exercise today?
- Did you say "no" and mean it?
- Were you brave?
- Did you speak your truth?
- Did you stick to a new routine?
- Did you choose faith over fear?

Celebrating the small wins is a tool that I keep towards the top of my mental health toolbox. Perspective is everything. Energy is everything. Let them match up to the best of your ability.

Time Out Strategy Session: Spend 10-15 minutes writing down everything you are grateful for. Nothing is too big or too small. If you need more room, use a separate piece of paper. *I suggest handwriting your list rather than typing it because the action of writing connects with your brain in a different way and allows you to have a better understanding.*

Mindset Shift #6: Nonattachment

Pain and loss are inevitable. Be the tree.

"Praise and blame, gain and loss, pleasure and sorrow come and go like the wind. To be happy, rest like a giant tree in the midst of them all." – Buddha

As humans, we are bound to experience both good times and bad times. It's an inescapable part of life. The giant tree that Buddha speaks of is symbolic because it remains rooted regardless of its environment. Being like the giant tree means letting the life around you—all of the things you can't control—happen while you remain steady and growing as the winds of life blow through your leaves. Now of course, you and I are not trees and we have this thing called emotions, but trees sway without falling, right? This mindset is about being flexible with nonattachment to whatever it is that is causing you pain and suffering.

If you're too attached to something that caused you pain (i.e., not letting go), you identify with pain as a part of who you are and your experience, and therefore may have a difficult time accepting good things into your life.

The most important part of this to understand is that nonattachment is not the same as ignoring. Detaching doesn't mean, *let me ignore this pain so that I detach from it and I feel better*. Quite the opposite. You can feel without letting it overtake your life, without beating yourself up, without questioning what you did to deserve that pain, and without reliving it over and over again. You don't have to wear your losses like a scar at the forefront of your everyday life.

I also want to note here that some trauma requires that you work with a mental health professional to process it. I strongly believe that deep trauma is not something anyone should have to heal from on his or her own. It's okay to ask someone for help watering your tree.

Detach from your worries.

Nonattachment can also be an important mindset shift for people who suffer from anxiety or worry endlessly. Most of the time, these worries stem from wanting something that you don't have or you are afraid you won't have. To better understand this, I want to go back to the Buddha quote above. The duality of opposites is a Buddhist principle called the Eight Worldly Winds in which each of the winds is a pair of opposite experiences. They are:

- Pleasure and Pain
- Gain and Loss
- Praise and Blame
- Fame and Shame

For example, people without jobs might be desperate to find one and people with jobs might be desperate for free time. Some people want to be famous and adored; some celebrities want anonymity and privacy. Athletes want to be champions; champions want less pressure. The point here is that whatever you are worried about or seeking to fulfill, someone is one the opposite end of where you are daydreaming about some form of what you have.

We are so attached to feeling and achieving pleasure, gain, praise, and fame—even more so in today's social media look at me I'm perfect, always happy, and successful society—that we feel that anything less is failure. Attachment to this ideology causes suffering because if you're too attached to being perfect and living an idealistic lifestyle, anything that doesn't equal up to that may cause suffering because you feel like a failure or unworthy. When you hold onto the ideas of who you should be so tightly that it causes anxiety, it might be because you identify with it so deeply that anything else in opposition causes suffering.

Here is another example: Every athlete wants to win, but some athletes are overly attached to winning. To these athletes, winning might mean something much deeper such as a way to win over a parent's approval or a way to support his or her family. In that instance, that motivation may cause suffering in several ways such as anxiety over anticipating a competition; loss of focus during the competition due to worry about not meeting the expectations of winning; or extreme pain or despair after a loss.

Be the tree. Be grounded and grow without worry because your roots are strong enough to withstand the rain and with the right nourishment, you'll continue to flourish. How can you do this? Recognize that the worries aren't your worries. They are coming from somewhere else and therefore they aren't yours to own. Just like the tree doesn't own the rain that falls on it, but instead, let's the drops of water roll of its leaves, branches, and trunk.

Time Out Strategy Session: What are some areas of your life that you can strengthen through nonattachment? Draw a picture of your tree. On the roots, trunk, branches and leaves, make notes of what your strengths are. Write down the things you are worried about in the sky or the ground, or wherever you like. They might just be words or they might be leaves, birds, clouds or whatever you like. Now, close your eyes and imagine that the wind is blowing the things that you are worried about around but your tree remains rooted, strong, and safe. Take note of how this feels.

Mindset Shift #7: Speaking up when you need help

Addressing your issues begins with self-awareness and clearing your mental space so that you can become more aware of what you're truly feeling. But, you don't have to figure it all out on your own. During tough times, healing and growth require that you vocalize what you need by having the humility to ask for help. Speaking with others can be a very powerful way to clear your mental space because the act of vocalization can help you gain perspective.

Whether you're 16 or 60, it's critical to talk to someone who you consider to be an adult adviser who is not a friend. Friends are of course great to talk to, but our peers sometimes can cloud the conversation because maybe you're not being totally upfront with them, or they're just telling you what they think you want to hear, or they don't have the experience to guide you on a specific issue.

What if my culture says it's weak to ask for help?

Time and time again, I've spoken with athletes who are resistant to getting help because they were taught to figure things on their own. In other words, you don't ask for help, you rely on yourself to get whatever it is that you want. And, if it's not what you want, you find a way to deal with it.

Whether it's due to the culture of the sport you play, your family beliefs, or your community, some athletes have learned to internalize everything. They may talk about their problems, but they don't really deal with the issue or find solutions for it. One reason being that, in the athlete's perspective, his or her self-reliance is a key in their success as an athlete. However, that same way of thinking doesn't translate perfectly outside of sports. A fact of life is that sometimes there are things that you need help with.

If you're struggling, be courageous enough to ask for help. There are people who will understand you and want to help you without judging you.

Throughout this Playbook, there are lots of exercises and worksheets, but these are just starting points. Mental wellness isn't a one-time DIY project. Yes, you have to take responsibility for your actions and choices to heal, but our minds and thoughts are complicated. There are innumerable benefits to speaking with someone who will listen and has the knowledge, tools, and training to help you actually deal with the problem and find a solution. This includes releasing stress by venting; finding new ways to look at a problem; gaining an understanding of what the issue is (e.g., anxiety, depression, OCD, PTSD, etc.); and identifying resolutions and an action plan healing. (Remember, if you can accept that you can heal your body, you can accept that you can heal your mind.)

Here's a list of people in your personal life that you can consider talking to:

- Parents
- Grandparents
- Aunts and Uncles
- Coaches
- Team Personnel such as the Player Development Coaches

- Mentors
- Teachers
- Religious Leaders

Whether over the phone, in person, or through a text message, you can open up the conversation by saying something like...

"This isn't easy for me to say, but I need help and you are someone that I trust. I am struggling with some inner stuff and I'm not sure where to start. Do you have some time to speak with me?"

You may also want to consider speaking with a therapist, sports psychologist, or other licensed mental health professional.

Time Out Strategy Session 1: What are you willing to do to get to where you want to be? What are you willing to do to feel inner peace and mental clarity? What if that meant putting your ego aside and speaking to someone?

> Time Out Strategy Session 2: Make a list of everyone in your life you can talk to and how you can best reach them (phone, text, in person, etc.). Then, in your own words, write down some things you can say when you need their help. You can use the example above as a starting place.

Mindset Shift #8: Breathe

Breathing is something that we do all day every day without really thinking about it. If you're an athlete, you might become aware of your breath if you're pushing so hard physically that your lungs hurt. If you're someone who deals with anxiety, you might become aware of your breath if you feel your heart racing during those infamous rough moments. If you're someone who meditates, you might become aware of your breath as a part of a breathing meditation. But, unless you have a reason to be aware of your breath, you're probably not thinking much about it. However, breathing may be just the break that your brain needs.

It's a concept that is so simple, yet often overlooked. I'll share a story about how this technique can be beneficial from the perspective of an athlete. One afternoon, I was speaking with a retired athlete who endured incredible struggles throughout his life. He saw sports as a way out of his problems and so he put everything into his sport, and he excelled. But, as all athletes will experience, one day you will retire from your full-time sports job regardless of the level you reach. And like many, many newly retired athletes, he had numerous life-altering and challenging obstacles to face and felt deep despair about what to do next. So, I asked him: What would you tell your younger self about mental wellness? What do you wish you knew back then? What would you tell a young athlete today?

He said, "Breathe." He wisely suggested that in stressful moments when you feel overwhelmed, give yourself the space process by giving yourself a few minutes to take a step back and breathe.

Why does breathing help your peace of mind? As stated by The American Institute of Stress, "Deep breathing increases the supply of oxygen to your brain and stimulates the parasympathetic nervous system, which promotes a state of calmness. Breathing techniques help you feel connected to your body—it brings your awareness away from the worries in your head and quiets your mind."[6]

There is much wisdom, perspective and calm to be found in taking a few minutes to step back and breathe.

Time Out Strategy Session: Try this breathing exercise.

- Breathe in positive energy. (Inhale slowly through your nose allowing your breath to fill your stomach.)
- Breathe out negative energy. (Exhale slowly through your nose feeling yourself becoming more relaxed as the tension leaves your body.)
- As you breathe, imagine that all of the stress you feel and everything that's weighing you down is floating away.
- Repeat three times for a total of four cycles.

Try this exercise for a week or two and see what you notice. Write down your observations.

Mindset Shift #9: Managing Expectations

Anxiety or stress due to expectations is extremely common. Expectations are ideas of what we believe will happen but yet are still unproven. Sometimes our expectations are conscious and sometimes they are unconscious. Sometimes expectations are projected from ourselves, and sometimes they are projected from other people and we adapt them. Reforming unconscious expectations aside, sometimes we experience stress or anxiety due to expectations that are right in front of our faces. The most common sources are from goals, other people, and ourselves.

Setting Healthy Expectations for Your Goals

Everyone has goals. Everyone needs goals. Even if your ideal situation is to sit still and do nothing, it's still an objective that you're wishing to obtain.

I really believe that among the biggest issues plaguing people today is the need for instant everything, but also the pressure to be more, do more, have more, and be this unicorn superhero version of yourself.

Here is one remedy for setting expectations for your goals… and you may not like it. Be patient. See it through and give yourself time to do so. Deadlines are great and all, but if they make you feel like failure or cause anxiousness, adjust your idea of your timeline. The days and weeks can be grueling and fleeting, yet the sum of your efforts adds up. You're likely to hit many, many blocks and "no's" on your way to wherever it is you're seeking to go.

No one plants a seed one day and expects a blooming, shady tree in a week. Our lives are like the rings on tree trunks. It takes time to grow and develop with proper nurturing. You might lose a branch here or there, but you'll be okay. You'll still grow. That's nature. That's life.

Setting Healthy Expectations with Other People

"I'm not in this world to live up to your expectations and you're not in this world to live up to mine." – Bruce Lee

We expect things of people and they expect things of us. Sometimes, those things don't match up. We can wind up feeling inadequate and frustrated. Truthfully, your success is not dependent on anyone else. Likewise, their success is not dependent on you. It's called free will.

It seems like a straightforward enough concept. However, the emotional ties are often what keep you in patterns. The emotional part can be tougher to breakthrough because no one wants to disappoint the people who they love and trust. Well, if they stop loving you, they don't deserve your love either.

On the other hand, if you have anxiety because you have a need to control people, places, and things, maybe it's time to examine what it would be like if you let go of that. Let's go back to the idea of free will.

Other people are responsible for their choices and actions, which means it's not a reflection of you. So, if they don't do or say what you would, that falls on them. You get to choose how much involvement you want in that relationship. Likewise, they get to choose if they want to continue to meet your expectations and what kind of involvement they want in a relationship with you too.

Whether you need to let go of the expectations you put on others, or you need to let go of the expectations others put on you, try repeating this affirmation: My life is mine.

Setting Healthy Expectations with Yourself

This one is my favorite topics. If you're like me, a lot of times your anxiety comes from being so hard on yourself. I don't know where my tough-gal complex originated. What I do know is sometimes it serves me well, but other times, I let it feed my ego and insecurities.

I expect myself to do everything and meet every expectation and be there for others and reach new goals. The webs of what I expect of myself are complex. It ranges widely and deeply from wanting everyone to be happy to proving myself as a business owner to giving my family my best to making sure my physical appearance is a certain way. And you know what happens when I chase these expectations obsessively? I lose focus of myself. Not only do I not feel grounded nor safe, I am literally depleted and I will spend an entire day sleeping trying to catch up. The resolution? You guessed it: a mindset shift.

You won't meet every expectation every day. That is such a hard pill to swallow but somewhere you have to find ways to accept that humans are imperfect beings with the best of intentions. It takes an effort to learn to love your self every day, which is where taking the time for self-care becomes so important.

Self-care is about setting healthy expectations for your routine. Try setting caring expectations in addition to all of the challenging ones. Here are some examples:

- I expect that I will keep my exercise schedule so that I can clear my head.
- I expect that I will take 15 minutes to take a bath on Monday nights to congratulate myself on making it through the first day of the week and to prepare for the rest of the week.
- I expect that I will put my phone away for date night.

- I expect that I will disconnect from technology at least two hours before bed.
- I expect that when I wake up in the morning, I will give myself an hour or two to get through my routine before I start answering text messages and emails.
- I expect that my brain can accept doing one thing a time.
- I expect to use meditation to help slow down my thoughts and bring me clarity.
- I expect myself to set space and time boundaries.
- I expect to have downtime several times a week to recharge.

Conversely, maybe you struggle with positivity. Here are some expectations you can try to adopt:

- I expect that I will do my best.
- I expect that things will always work out in the end.
- I expect that everything will be okay again.
- I expect that if I put in the effort, I will see results, no matter how slowly.
- I expect to love myself.

See where I'm going with all of this? If you're stressed or anxious or struggling with mental wellness, take time to think about what are you expecting and how that is affecting how you feel.

Time Out Strategy Session: What are some healthy expectations that you can set for your goals, other people, and yourself? Write them down in the space below.

Mindset Shift #10: Overcoming a Fear of Making Mistakes

Many athletes seek answers on how to overcome a fear of making mistakes in sports. As we addressed in Chapter Five, there are many different reasons why an athlete might fear making a mistake. Sometimes that fear, however, can be immobilizing causing the individual to freeze up or retreat from his or her sport all together.

> *"I've missed more than 9,000 shots in my career. I've lost almost 300 games. Twenty-six times, I've been trusted to take the game winning shot and missed. I've failed over and over and over again in my life. And that is why I succeed." – Michael Jordan*

Overcoming a fear of making mistakes starts with reframing your mindset around your fears. Maybe you're thinking something like, *I know that pro athletes and successful people make lots of mistakes, but no matter how hard I try, I can't shake my own fears. My mistakes are mine and therefore they are personal.* To help you move past this, you first have to make the decision that you are wiling to be imperfect on your way to reaching your end game. I'm not expecting that once you make this declaration that your fears will be completely gone, but I imagine that you'll begin to become a little braver as you focus on your motivation.

For the next step, as you work on reframing your mindset, create thought habits to match your goals. Below are some perspectives and affirmations you can begin with. You can use these, edit them, or create your own. I encourage you to make them as personal as possible so that you connect with them strongly in a positive way that hits home.

Sample Perspectives:

- When someone puts pressure on me to be perfect or is overly critical of my mistakes, it originates from their insecurities and has nothing to do with me. I don't own anyone else's insecurities or failures.
- Think of the person you most admire. Do they make mistakes? Yes.
- You can make mistakes, shake it off, and keep going all in an instant.

- Practice being here in the moment, not the past or the future. Be here now, feeling secure, clear, and calm.
- Would you rather not make a mistake or spend your life wondering what would have happened if you tried?

Sample Affirmations:

- Every single person makes mistakes. I'm human, not a robot.
- Mistakes are proof that I'm trying.
- Perfection doesn't guarantee success. Mistakes don't guarantee failure.
- The ground underneath me is safe for me to walk on.
- I can laugh at my mistakes and roll with them.

Overcoming a Fear of Making Mistakes with Visualization

The next mindset shift tool I'll share with you is visualization. For starters, visualize yourself living your goal using sight, sound, smell, vision, etc. to make that vision come to life right now. Feel it being real in this moment. Imagine how amazing it will feel when you achieve your goal.

For athletes who are afraid of tryouts, practices, or games, imagine yourself in the situation in which you have to perform. You're completely and clearly focused. You're in the zone. It's as if there is no one watching you. You perform at your best. Even if you make a mistake, it doesn't interrupt your flow. You glide right through it performing at your best completely clear and undistracted. And when it's over, you feel wholly accomplished.

One of the reasons that visualization is so powerful is that you realistically experience the situation so that when you are actually there, it feels more like déjà vu making it easier for you to live it. On top of building belief in yourself, it's also like you're building a positive been there, done that type of confidence.

Take it one step at a time

As you work on changing your perspective from a fear-based mentality to a strength-based mentality, try not to spend too much time in your thoughts. Taking action is extremely important because this is where you'll put your thought habits and visualizations to work. If taking action is overwhelming, begin with small, manageable goals.

Time Out Strategy Session 1: What are your next steps towards overcoming a fear? How and when will you do this?

Time Out Strategy Session 2: Dr. Wayne Dyer said, "When you change the way you look at things, the things you look at change." Are you still feeling stuck on something? Try looking at it from different perspectives. Write down the situation and then write down different perspectives. Pretend you're the other person involved, a friend/confidant, a stranger, and see what perspectives emerge. It may not change your situation, but it can help you understand it better.

CHAPTER ELEVEN

PLAY #5 – BALANCING SPORTS & LIFE

Everyone can relate to the feeling of pressure. Athletes, in particular, feel a constant need to somehow strike a balance between sports and life. This pressure can cause mental health issues to arise because there is a multitude of components that get squeezed into sports and life at all levels. There's surely always something going on, which makes balancing sports and life tough.

Being an active player at any level is an incredible gift that I think most athletes cherish, but it's not always a pretty day-to-day road that they travel.

Pressures on Student Athletes

At the most rudimentary level all the way through college, student athletes face their own set of pressures. Many people assume that younger athletes play only for fun because it's not yet a "job." Well, that may be true, but athletes face a ton of expectations to develop faster and stronger than ever before, particularly if they want to advance to the next level of his or her sport, and that pressure only increases as they move forward.

Add this to having to mature and develop as an individual while having to achieve certain accolades in school, maintain healthy relationships with family and peers, travel for games, develop a personal brand for college and beyond, earn stellar star ratings, endure financial pressure, and do it all under the public eye, it's no wonder that more and more athletes are coming forward with mental health issues.

Pressures on Pro Athletes

Pro athletes have the obvious pressure of playing at the top level, developing their sports IQ, getting along with teammates, dealing with media, and the incredibly strenuous training, travel, and playing schedule that goes along with it. Not only are pro athletes expected to play at a certain level, they are also expected to be healthy and take as much care as possible not to get injured. And if they are injured, that adds a whole new level of pressure to get back on the court or field. On top of it all, everything that they lay their bodies on the line for is just a business and they might feel more like a commodity than a person.

Outside of their time with the team, pro athletes might also have a family and kids who depend on them and want to spend time with them; financial decisions that affect their future and the future of those they love; being a role model; social media chatter; life after sports; and so on and so on.

Balancing Sports and Life

Pressure in life never stops because we all have to do things that aren't always easy to do in order to get the things we want and need. For athletes, balancing sports and life can feel impossible at times. What you can do is use a combination of action, mindset, and self-care to align all of your priorities to the best of your ability. Even though they all intertwine with one another, they can each be addressed individually to create a holistic plan.

Here's how to create more balance...

1. Action – First and foremost it's important to realize that the world, and our lives, will never be perfectly balanced. There will always be something that you spend more time on than other things simply because that's where your focus and energy requires you to be in order to achieve what it is that you want to achieve.

If, however, you're feeling off balance, here are some questions you can ask yourself:

- What are my most important goals right now?
- What are my priorities?
- Do my goals and my priorities match up?
- Where am I spending the majority of my time?
- How is that benefitting me?
- What am I doing to quiet my mind and relax my body?
- In what area(s) do I feel like I'm not spending enough time?
- Why do I feel that way? Who or what is causing me to feel that way?
- If I were to take one thing off of my plate in order to achieve my goals, what would that be?
- If I were to say "no" to one thing in order to gain more balance in my schedule, what would that be?

Asking questions like these can help you gain insight into what action you need to take, even if that action is to eliminate something. Remember: Never, ever, sacrifice your self-care time. No one ever said that you had to sacrifice and struggle 24/7 in order to achieve your goal. Just as we discussed in the previous chapter, your body needs rest to repair and so does your mind.

2. Mindset – Imbalance and pressure are a part of the world we live in. Spiritually speaking, you can theoretically reach a place where you are unbothered by anyone or anything. I'm not discouraging that practice, however, no one is perfect and in life, feelings of pressure and imbalance are completely normal.

You might not be able to escape feeling pressure at all times, but you can choose what you want to do with it. The awesome thing about mindset is that you get to choose your perspective. A mental health professional can help you work through discovering and breaking negative thought patterns as well as developing new thought patterns.

We'll do some work with negative thought habits as an exercise later in this Playbook. For now, here is a series of questions you can ask yourself when you feel pressure:

- Who/what is putting pressure on me?
- What is causing me the most stress?
- Why am I allowing it?
- What if I choose to not let that pressure me?
- What would that look like? How would that feel?
- What do I want instead?
- How can I still pursue my goals and manage stress/pressure?
- What can I do to achieve that?

Keep in mind that mindset and action might include saying, "no," which many people don't do because they fear letting someone down. The person you say "no" to may not love it initially, but they'll get over it. You're the only one who has to live your life.

3. Self-care – In the "action" section above, I mentioned self-care. This is imperative to balance. I wholeheartedly believe in attacking any problem from the inside out meaning that if you feel unbalanced, the resolution begins from within.

The key is that no one can do that for you. You can't outsource self-care. Suffering is not a badge of honor. (To clarify, I don't mean suffering as a victim in an uncontrolled circumstance, I mean suffering due to choices you make because you think life has to be hard to be successful.) Be protective of your self-care and disciplined about personal development, which, again, includes breaks and believe it or not, doing nothing to clear your mind.

If you're having trouble with your self-care (hint: you feel lost and pulled in a million directions), ask yourself the following questions:

- What places or activities make me feel the most relaxed?
- What would I like to improve on with myself?
- How can more self-care time help support that?
- Where in my schedule can I block out a time to do nothing but relax and rest?
- If I had to add one self-care task to my schedule every week, what would that be?
- If I had to add one self-care task to my schedule every day, what would that be?
- Who can hold me accountable for taking time for my self-care?
- What might my life look like if I took more time for self-care? How would I feel?
- Why is my self-care worth the time investment?

CHAPTER TWELVE

PLAY #6 – MINDFULNESS & MEDITATION

Mindfulness and meditation are a secret weapon that a myriad of highly successful athletes use. For example, Google "NBA players" and "meditation" and see what pops up.

Did you know that studies show we take between 17,000 and 23,000 breaths per day[7] and, on average, have between 12,000 to 60,000 thoughts per day[8]? That means that most of the time our thoughts are moving faster than we are breathing! This is one of the main reasons we use focused breathing, meditation, and mindful movement as a tool in mental wellness. It is the fastest and most effective ways to slow down our heart rate, breath, and thoughts.

So why isn't mindfulness and meditation talked about more often in sports? For starters, there's the whole culture of having to appear to be extraordinarily tough. Athletes might be afraid that they will be viewed as wishy-washy or ridiculed if they break out into a meditation in the locker room. Others might feel like they are already in control of their thoughts. Another reason is simply the fact that most athletes have never heard of nor been introduced to mindfulness and meditation.

What is mindfulness?

Mindfulness is living in the moment and being fully focused on the present without concern of the past or the future. It is a mindset of heightened awareness that creates a gap among emotions, thoughts, and reactions in a nonattached manner. The individual is completely connected to mind, body, and soul. In this space, the person experiences heightened self-awareness, mental clarity, focus, and inner peace.

Mindfulness helps you become simultaneously clear and connected in such an effortless, unrestricted way that you are one with where you are at, unmoved by outside circumstances with the keen awareness of what is happening in the moment, and the ability to anticipate what is coming. It's an energetic connection with what is unseen by everyone else that is led by ego alone.

Benefits of mindfulness and meditation for Athletes:

- Heightened self-awareness
- Know yourself and be way more in tune with your body
- Find balance in mind, body, and spirit
- Manage pressure/stress/anxiety
- Improve your focus and concentration by training your mind to block out the noise
- Strengthen your instinct by clearing your mind to listen
- Balance emotions so you are steady in high and low moments
- Achieve crystal clear clarity in the moment during games
- Let each moment flow without looking too far ahead or dwelling on past plays

How to implement mindfulness and meditation into your routine:
Give yourself quiet alone time every day even if it's just for 10 or 15 minutes. Use this time to clear your head and let everything going on around you float away. Choose a space that's comfortable for you. You may want to turn off the lights and play meditative music (there are lots of options for this on YouTube).

The easiest way to clear your mind is through meditation. Meditation can be done in a variety of different ways because the goal isn't to sit still until you start levitating or some other supernatural thing you might have seen on TV; the goal is to simply gently let go of all expectations and thoughts.

Here are four types of meditation you can try:

1. Focused Breathing
In this type of meditation, you focus on your breath. That's literally all it is. One way to do this as I learned from meditation guru, davidji, is to inhale slowly counting to four, hold that breath counting to four, exhale slowly counting to four, and then hold that out breath counting to four. If you do this four times, you will have completed a one-minute meditation, which is easy enough for any beginner. You can even focus on a word like "peace" with each inhale and exhale. Increase your time a little bit each week as you make it a part of your daily routine. The results will begin to show.

2. Mindful Movement
This is one of my favorite exercises, particularly in meditation for athletes. I practice mindful movement before I sit to meditate. This is because I'm a very active person, so to go from 100 to zero is nearly impossible. Before I start my sitting meditation,

I spend some time doing mindful movements because it gives my body and mind a way to move together and begin the process of slowing down by flowing together.

Here is an example of a mindful movement that you can try.
Stand with your arms at your side. Inhale slowly while lifting your arms up over your head slowly. Pause here for a moment. Exhale slowly while bringing your arms back down. I like to imagine that as my arms float up, I'm gaining strength, clarity, and peace. As my arms float down to my side, all tension, worry, and stress is leaving as my jaw, my shoulders and my body become more relaxed. Repeat this movement set eight times.

3. Guided Meditation
Guided meditations can be found in apps, on YouTube, or in person at meditation classes or one-on-one with a coach. You can even write your own! The advantage of this type of meditation is that you'll listen to someone's voice guiding you through the exercise, which can be extremely helpful when you first start practicing or when you want help directing your mind.

Here is a guided relaxation meditation you can try:
I encourage you to listen to the recording via the link below or read it aloud and record it on your phone. This way you focus on the meditation and not on reading what's next.

Visit PurposeSoulAthletics.com/Playbook-Meditation. Use password PlaybookMeditation.

Find a quiet space. Choose to sit or lay down. Close your eyes. Set an intention to relax and clear some space in your mind. Let's begin.

- Inhale slowly.
- Exhale slowly.
- Continue inhaling and exhaling slowly.
- Begin to let go of everything on your mind, just breathe.
- Feel the space in your mind open up as you continue to release everything weighing on your mind with each calming breath.
- With each breath feel your thoughts getting lighter and tension leaving your jaws, then your shoulders, and then your body all the way down to your toes.
- Now imagine that each breath is a light, peaceful energy flowing through your body allowing you to feel calmer… more at peace… more relaxed…

- Feel this same light calming your mind, slowing down your thoughts, allowing you to let go of everything that doesn't serve you in this moment.
- Continue inhaling and exhaling slowly allowing any distracting thoughts or noises to simply float away for the moment. It's normal to have a lot of thoughts when you meditate. Don't fight them. Just let them float away.
- Let yourself feel relaxed, forgiving, loving, confident, happy, and free.
- Let each breath guide you to total relaxation as peace floats around you and through you.
- As you continue to breathe, enjoy the miraculous life running through you in your breath.
- Continue breathing for a few more moments enjoying this place of peace and clarity.
- When you're ready, begin to open your eyes focusing on a point in the room, waking up, but knowing you can always return this place of relaxation and just be.

> Time Out Strategy Session: Journal about anything you noticed about how you felt before the meditation and afterwards as well as note anything you noticed during the meditation. Keep in mind that each time you meditate, you may feel different because each day of our lives is different.

4. Affirmations During Exercise

Athletes might be surprised to learn that you can meditate during your strength training routine. Remember, meditation and mindfulness are based on focusing on something specific in the moment. My favorite time to sneak in meditative thinking is to use affirmations during tough, but motionless exercises such as when holding a plank. I hate holding planks for a long time so to pass the time, I repeat affirmations and envision my dream life, the goal that I'm working towards, while holding the plank position. This is helpful because I'm able to hold the plank for a longer period of time, but also because I'm focusing and clearing my mind, which is a meditative act.

Bonus Tip: Two keys to meditation:

1. No matter which style of meditation that you try, the first key is to let go of all expectations. Don't worry about what you're supposed to be feeling or if you're doing it right or not. Meditation is a judgment-free space. You may experience something different in each meditation or nothing at all, either way, you're doing it correctly.
2. The second key is let go of your thoughts. It's perfectly normal for thoughts to come into your mind during your practice. Don't get frustrated; it's part of the process. When you notice your mind trailing off, simply pause and gently watch your thoughts float away knowing that you can always come back to whatever is on your mind after your meditation.

CHAPTER THIRTEEN

PLAY #7 – SOCIAL MEDIA STRATEGY

In January 2008, I opened my first business with a focus on content writing and digital marketing, specializing in social media marketing. This was at a time when social media was in its infancy and it hadn't caught on as a mainstream way to advertise one's business. Since then, social media has completely disrupted the field of marketing, but it's also completely changed our personal lives.

For most of us, social media is a complex space that magnifies on a grander scale two contradictory aspects of human nature: we want to be praised and it hurts when people are critical.

Social media is a lonely place. Sometimes, it feels like you're talking to a wall. And sometimes, that can flare up insecurities particularly when you feel like your voice isn't being heard offline or online.

Social media is a dizzying place. It's confusing. *What should I post? What shouldn't I post? Did I say something wrong or dumb? How can I get more people to like me and see me? Look what so-and-so posted. Why can't I be more like that? Why does this person need so much attention? How do I not take it personally when someone is being a hater? Why am I not more popular? Why do people care so much about what I post anyway? Who are these people commenting trolling my stuff?* The range of emotions is vast. It can be overwhelming.

Everywhere we look in the media, athletes, and even entertainers, are coming forward saying that they are taking breaks from social media for a variety of mental health reasons. Study after study is being conducted on the relationship between social media usage and mental health problems. Make no mistake: social media can not only impact your mental wellness, but also the quality of your life if you don't know how to manage it.

You may think that you're someone who doesn't care about what other people have to say, but in reality, someone, somewhere will say something that will hit an emotional nerve. We all have buttons that can be pushed for better or for worse.

Social media is a business. Treat it that way.

For athletes, social media can be a recruiting tool and a way to elevate his or her brand. However, this public display and public access comes with a price. In my agency, we constantly speak to businesses about social media strategy, which includes not only branding and content, but also how to manage social network communities and comments. This same strategy can apply to individuals. Regardless of your age or playing level, make a resolution to use social media responsibly. I urge you to create a strategy not just for managing your brand, but also for managing your usage and approach.

Here are a few tips that can help:

1. Be strategic about what you post:

- Protect the integrity of your personal brand. Create a set of criteria that your posts need to meet. For example, the post showcases who you are as an athlete and a human.
- Before you post something, make a deal with yourself that you will not evaluate your self-worth based on likes and comments that you get from that post.
- You can't take back the things you post. Even when you delete the post, maybe someone took a screenshot or has a way of searching through archives.
- Never, ever post when you're emotional unless you are prepared to manage both positive and negative comments. As an alternative, there are other apps and forums where you can vent in a healthier environment.
- Reiterate to yourself that everything you post is a reflection of you. No one expects you to be perfect, but not everything you think needs to be said in a public space.
- If you really want to participate in a controversial conversation, ask yourself these questions first:
    - Will participating in this help me feel better?
    - Is this worth my mental and emotional energy?
    - Do I feel so strongly about this subject that it will be easy for me shake off negative feedback without getting emotionally involved?
- If you're not sure if you want to post something or not, save it as a draft in your phone (not on the network) and go back a few hours or even a day later to see how you feel about it.

2. Integrate social media disconnect time into your training routine:

- Take technology breaks. The Fear of Missing Out (FOMO) seems to become more of an obsession the more connected someone is. Set rules for how often you'll look at social networks and during what hours you'll do so. Create time and space for mental breaks. Being present in the moment and disconnected from technology can be an incredibly refreshing reality check. For example, after a certain time in the evening, I don't look at my phone unless it rings. Sometimes, I'll put my phone on Do Not Disturb so that I'll only get alerts in an emergency.
- If you're feeling exceptionally burnt out or you're going through a difficult time, consider deleting your social media apps from your phone for a week or two. Remove the temptation and give yourself time to focus on yourself and heal. You don't have to announce on social media that you're taking a break either. Just do it.
- Consider this disconnect a part of your disciplined training in focus. Training yourself to focus off of the field or court is as important as the training you do to prepare yourself to focus during game time.

3. Be mindful of your online circle.

You've likely heard that it's important to be mindful of the company you keep. Well, that extends to social media, too.

- Follow accounts that make you feel good and inspire you. Get rid of everything that makes you feel bad or like you're not enough.
- Block the trolls and never engage with them. Everything you post is a reflection of you regardless of who started it.
- Keep in mind that you don't have to be the social media police. Don't engage in negative comments or conversations. That will only drain your brain energy and distract you from what you really need to focus on in your life. It's also highly unlikely that you're going to change anyone's mind so it's really not worth risking your mental and emotional energy.
- Remember: There are people who are so unhappy in their own lives that they will never hesitate to post something negative about you or someone you love. For others, it's entertaining to push buttons (literally and figuratively). Their comments aren't a reflection of you; their comments are a reflection of the individual leaving the comment.

> *"What other people think of me is none of my business. One of the highest places you can get to is being independent of the good opinions of other people."* – Dr. Wayne Dyer

If you need a social media presence for your brand, consider hiring someone to manage it for you. You can ask to approve posts before they are shared. The advantage here is that you won't be tempted to look at comments and replies if that is something affecting your mental wellness.

CHAPTER FOURTEEN

PLAY #8 – MENTAL WELLNESS WORKSHEETS

Throughout the Playbook so far, we've looked at some of the most critical reasons for developing a strong mental health routine and even what to do when you feel like your mental health is unbalanced. In this chapter, I'm providing a few worksheets to help you further put mental wellness into practice. This isn't about perfection; this is about ongoing self-awareness to improve your mental wellness. The principles and exercises presented through this Playbook are meant to help heighten your self-awareness and expand your mental wellness. The exercises can also be a complement to what you are working on in therapy or with a coach.

Exercise 1: Athlete Mental Wellness Zone Part 1

What is the Mental Wellness Zone?

For athletes, the zone is a sweet spot of clearing your mind and to allow everything to flow in unison undeterred by outside circumstances. In the zone, you attack your game with trust, purpose, and laser focus. You are intuitively responsive, rather than emotionally reactive. You trust that your body and mind are prepared from all of the hours you spent training and will instinctively act in unison during game time.

Your mental wellness zone is similar to your game-time zone except that it's something you work to develop and integrate into your daily life. As we have talked about throughout this Playbook, your emotions will tell you everything you need to know. Learning to understand and identify your emotions and reactions can help you check-in with yourself and know when you need to adjust something. Use the following chart to check-in with yourself at any given moment to see where you are in your mental wellness zone.

Exercise 2: Mental Wellness Zone Part 2

Use this questionnaire at any time to get an idea of where you're at in the Mental Wellness Zone. Base your answers on the last 1-2 weeks of your life.

1. Have you traveled from one destination to the next without remembering part of or the entire journey?
   - Yes
   - No

2. Have you lost sleep thinking about something?
   - Yes
   - No

3. Have you worried about the unknown?
   - Yes
   - No

4. Have you overacted to something? (E.g., explosive emotion)
   - Yes
   - No

5. Have you let a coach, teammate, opponent or other person negatively get in your head?
   - Yes
   - No

6. Have you overanalyzed something in the past?
   - Yes
   - No

7. Have you doubted yourself?
   - Yes
   - No

8. Have you had an emotional outburst?
   - Yes
   - No

9. Have you lost motivation or given up?
   - ❏ Yes
   - ❏ No

10. Have you gotten distracted during a game or practice?
    - ❏ Yes
    - ❏ No

11. Have you said, "I don't care," when you really did care?
    - ❏ Yes
    - ❏ No

12. Have you struggled to get out of bed?
    - ❏ Yes
    - ❏ No

13. Have you had racing thoughts?
    - ❏ Yes
    - ❏ No

14. Have you felt anger, sadness or other negative emotion for a long stretch of time?
    - ❏ Yes
    - ❏ No

15. Have you felt like people are out to get you or everyone is against you?
    - ❏ Yes
    - ❏ No

16. Have you thought about something unpleasant and buried it in the back of your mind?
    - ❏ Yes
    - ❏ No

17. Have you felt off balance?
    - ❏ Yes
    - ❏ No

18. Were you too afraid to say how you feel so you didn't?
    - ❏ Yes
    - ❏ No

19. Did something on social media get into your head or distract you in a negative way?
    - Yes
    - No

20. Did you say, "yes" to something that didn't feel right to you?
    - Yes
    - No

20. Did you use your sport as the primary outlet for anger or other issue in your life?
    - Yes
    - No

How did you do? The more "no's," you got, the more in the Mental Wellness Zone you are.

Exercise 3: Understanding Your "Here and Now"

We've talked a lot about self-awareness. Your "here and now" relates to where you are in your life at this moment. The next exercise will help you explore specific areas of your life. When you think of each of these areas of your life, how do they feel? What emotions come up as your first reaction? Write down your first emotion about each area of your life in the boxes below. There are no right or wrong answers.

Sports	School/Work	Social Life	Alone Time	Family
Immediate Goals	Future Goals	Mindset	Physical Body	Spiritual
Finances	Relationships	Health	Career	Social Media

Looking at the chart above, what, if anything, stands out to you?

On a scale of 1-10 (10 being the most important), rate each of these areas according to the priority they take in your life right now.

Which of these areas can you celebrate and feel accomplished in?

Which of these areas would you like to work on more?

Exercise 4: Becoming Aware of Thought Habits

As we've discovered throughout this Playbook, thoughts can affect a variety of areas in your life. Oftentimes, our thoughts are so habitual that we are unaware of them.

Spend some time over the next week observing any negative thought habits that come up. Then, use the space below to write them down and create new ones that you can adopt. Remember, this is a process that takes time. It requires discipline to break a negative habit and replace it with a healthy one. It may also require that you heal deeply-rooted wounds. Your new thought habit should be something that makes you feel happy, peaceful, confident, and hopeful. As you begin to change your thought habits, you'll probably notice your actions match your new mindset.

Negative Thought Habit	Positive Thought Habit
Example 1: Good things never happen. Example 2: I'm afraid of making a mistake. Example 3: I will probably fail.	Example 1: I am blessed right now. Example 2: Everyone who succeeds makes mistakes. Example 3: I am prepared for opportunities.

Exercise 5: Create Positive Affirmations

When coaching athletes and professionals, the topic of incorporating positive affirmations into his or her mental wellness routine inevitably comes up. One of the factors that makes mental health tribulations so frustrating is that it can be difficult to break the negative thought and emotional patterns because it requires a mindset shift, and sometimes healing. This is not always an easy or quick process, particularly when you developed the thought habits with the intention of keeping yourself "safe."

Just like in the previous exercise, positive affirmations are a tool that I've found to be very helpful. When you identify a negative thought, you need a way to turn that around by consciously choosing a new thought. Affirmations allow you to focus on a positive thought over and over again, which can help create a shift in your mind and subsequently your emotions and/or even your body. Again, keep in mind that while affirmations are an effective tool, to really be successful, you'll have to work on the things that caused you to create the negative thought habits in the first place.

Here are some examples of mental health affirmations:

Athletic Mental Health Affirmations:

- I am confident in my athletic abilities.
- I play with confidence whether in practice or in a game.
- My mind and body are stronger each day.
- My mind and body are fearless.
- There are no limits to what I can accomplish.
- I excel under pressure.
- My teammates and coaches can count on me.
- It is easy for me to find my zone.
- It is easy to rely on instinct and on my teammates.
- The past is in the past. I play in the present.
- Being compensated for my gifts puts me in a position to share more of my gifts.
- I act without expectations. I do what makes my soul feel good and fulfilled.
- I can learn new skills at any time I choose.
- Every season happens one day at a time. Enjoy the moment.
- Mistakes are proof that I'm trying and learning.

Everyday Affirmations:

- It is safe for me to speak my truth.
- Good things are happening.
- I can succeed on any path I choose.
- My body, mind, and soul flow together in unison.
- I have a prosperous mindset.
- I am limitless.
- I can and I am.
- I am doing my best.
- I trust myself to make the right decisions.
- I let go of the things that no longer serve me.
- The more gratitude I give, the better I feel and the more I receive.

Affirmations for Healing in Hard Times:

- I am healing and becoming the best version of myself.
- It is okay to take the time to heal.
- I give myself permission to go easy on myself.
- I give myself permission to heal.
- There is nothing permanently wrong with me. Everything is temporary.
- I surround myself with people who are understanding, caring, and loving. I am open to their support.
- I love myself even with my flaws. I'm only human.
- Even when I'm hurting, I know it'll pass and I'll be okay.
- It is possible to heal and be happy.
- Every day I heal a little more.
- Everything will be okay again.
- I deserve to be happy.
- I forgive in order to let go of anger.

Use the space below to create your own affirmations:

Exercise 6: Putting it Together

1. What did you learn about yourself from the exercises so far?

2. In what areas can you improve your mental wellness?

3. What's one step you can take to help improve your mental wellness?

4. What can you ask for help with? Who can you ask to help you?

5. What, if anything, else did you observe?

CHAPTER FIFTEEN

PLAY #9 – HOW TO SUPPORT SOMEONE GOING THROUGH MENTAL HEALTH ISSUES

Having watched other people struggle with mental illness disorders through various points in my life, I can appreciate how it can be challenging to understand what's going on when you're not the person who is suffering. Even if you've personally experienced mental health issues, while you might be more empathetic, you'll probably still have to step outside of yourself, and remove your emotion and perspective to be there for him or her. It can be complicated.

If you find yourself trying to support someone who is struggling with a mental health issue you may feel helpless. However, here are some ways that you can offer support.

- They will probably be scared. Let them know that it's okay to be scared. It is a scary thing to go through, but things will get better and you'll be there for them.
- Let them know that they are not alone because mental health issues can feel overwhelmingly isolating and lonely.
- Let them know that you appreciate them and love them.
- Tell them that you understand that it must be really difficult and that you support them.
- If they make a mistake or have a bad day, assure them that it's ok and they will be ok. Even if there isn't a quick fix, everything always works out somehow. Life is complicated, but hardships can be a moment in time if they are managed correctly.

- If they need to talk, listen with empathy. The person may not want advice, but rather someone to just listen and try to understand them.
- Let them know that you're not angry.
- Let them know that you don't think of them differently.
- Share with them that you admire them for being honest about their struggles and that you're honored to listen.
- Help them make an appointment with a licensed mental health professional and offer to take them there. Again, it can be really scary for the person to do that on his or her own. By offering to help with that, it can bring them some comfort and relieve some of the pressure and anxiety of getting help.
- Be patient and know that the best thing you can do is be supportive and understanding.
- Understand that the individual has to want to get help and even then, it's a long road with plenty of ups and downs.
- Know that it's neither your fault nor your 100% responsibility. Feeling guilty will only make the other person feel worse. Encouraging them to do certain things can definitely help, but it may also mean they are doing those things to appease you. Remember, there's no one clear cure-all and it's a process. Don't give up, but also don't put all of the blame on yourself.
- Always keep trying and always let them know that you are fighting with them, but understand that you can only do your best.
- Take care of yourself because the first rule of any kind of caregiving is to first take care of your own health and balance.

Whatever method you choose, support them through words and through actions. It's a delicate balance and you may find that you're repeating yourself, but to that person, who only wants to feel normal again, when you offer a balance of support and normalcy, it can only help to feel that someone gets them, is supporting them, and that their voice is being heard without judgment.

CHAPTER SIXTEEN

PLAY # 10 – TEAM MENTAL WELLNESS EVALUATION

Teams are made up of individuals and those individuals change from time-to-time. Therefore, it's crucial to have a mental wellness plan in place that has a strong foundation but is also fluid.

Here are a few questions you can answer to get started:

- Does every player and coach know who to go to, and have the contact information for that individual, when they have a mental wellness issue?
- Does every player and coach know how to handle personal mental wellness outside of the team?
- Do players and coaches have access to psychologists, psychiatrists, or other mental health professionals?
- Do they have access to ongoing training in topics such as mindfulness, meditation, and emotional intelligence?
- Does the team have mental wellness training standards that are defined as clearly as physical strength training standards are?
- Is there a system for returning and new player support? This can happen organically through relationships that veterans form with new team members, but it's really helpful to identify leaders who are willing to step up in the mental wellness advocate role.
- Is there a mental health professional available during practices and on game days?
- Is there someone in the organization who is responsible for regularly checking in with players individually by asking questions like, "How are you" and "What's new?"

5W1H of Team Mental Wellness

- **Who** is in charge of mental wellness in your organization? Who are the contacts for mental wellness?
- **What** is at stake by not addressing mental wellness? What are the advantages of addressing mental wellness? What are the issues that your team is facing right now that could affect mental wellness? If a player, coach, or personnel has a mental health emergency, what is the plan?
- **Why** is mental wellness important to your team? This can tie into your "why" for whatever your goal for the year is and/or to whatever your mission is as an organization.
- **When** will you implement mental wellness training? When will mental wellness be offered? When will players have access to mental wellness training? For example, will it be during practices, off-hours, etc.?
- **Where** will players and coaches go when they have an issue? Where will mental health and wellness training be offered?
- **How** will mental wellness be offered to players and coaches?

CHAPTER SEVENTEEN

THE FINAL BUZZER

"Mental health isn't just an athlete thing. What you do for a living doesn't have to define who you are. This is an everyone thing. No matter what our circumstances, we're all carrying around things that hurt—and they can hurt us if we keep them buried inside." – Kevin Love[9]

For some people, mental health issues pop up and catch them by surprise. For others, maintenance is the key to managing an ongoing mental health issue and there is no finality to it. Likewise, a person may never experience a mental illness, but they will have emotions and experiences that require healing. Regardless of the scenario, when mental wellness becomes an issue, it requires our respect and attention. It can be a battle that feels insurmountable at times, but it can also present the greatest opportunity for learning and growth.

> As long as we have thoughts and feelings, there will never be a finish line in mental wellness. You can't retire from being a human.

I don't know what causes some people to struggle with mental health more than others because the complexity of the mind makes it nearly impossible to pinpoint a specific answer, especially because each person is unique in their genetic makeup, upbringing, and experiences—I like to think of these components as layers. What I do know is that athletes are humans with extraordinary physical talent and resolve. If an athlete can approach his or her self-development holistically—mind, body, and soul—they will set themselves up for success as an athlete and in every other area of their life.

Because mental health is supremely intricate, personal, and at times complicated, it would be impossible to address every issue and resolution in this Playbook.

However, you now have some tools to consider as you begin to develop your mental wellbeing, which is the greatest strength an athlete can acquire.

What to do next:

- Give yourself room to breathe and to check-in with yourself. Be disciplined about taking time for yourself to practice self-awareness and self-reflection regularly.
- Practice meditation and breathing exercises daily to help create the mental space to clear your mind, balance emotions, practice affirmations, visualize outcomes, etc.
- Repeat your affirmations first thing in the morning and as the last thing before you fall asleep.
- Remind yourself to be mindful of your perspective and your self-talk.
- Vocalize when something feels off. Reach out to someone who is qualified to support you such as a therapist, coach, religious leader, etc. You do not have to heal on your own. You are not alone.
- If you're a coach, have a mental health and wellness plan for your team that is clearly and regularly communicated to players.

If you're interested in learning more about mental wellness coaching or workshops for you or your team, please contact Misty at misty@faithlovejourney.com. For more athlete mental wellness resources, please visit purposesoulathletics.com.

ABOUT THE AUTHOR

Misty Buck is a certified Professional Life Coach (CPC), Spiritual Life Coach (CSC), and business owner. Growing up as the coach's daughter and a cheerleader, Misty spent countless hours in the world of sports and around athletes where she learned that your value was largely determined by your ability to be tough in any and every situation. Don't cry. Don't be a baby. Walk it off. However, as a shy and sensitive kid, Misty had extreme difficulty in dealing with various painful and traumatic events that occurred during her childhood and into her twenties. Her internal struggle with mental health eventually exploded, and she soon realized that her emotions were real no matter how much shame she felt for feeling them, and or how hard she tried to walk it off. However, Misty also realized that she could dig into her competitive athletic spirit to face her mental health struggles head-on through honesty, humility, and grit. She learned how to use a holistic mind, body, and soul approach to healing and daily living to cultivate inner peace and clarity. As a Coach, Misty has a passion for guiding athletes to enjoy mental wellness through holistic action. In addition to her coaching credentials, Misty also holds a Bachelor of Arts degree in Communication (Public Relations) and English (Creative Writing) from Florida State University where she graduated Cum Laude.

www.purposesoulathletics.com
@TheMistyBuck

REFERENCES

1. NAMI Mental Health By The Numbers. (n.d.). Retrieved July 17, 2019, from https://www.nami.org/Learn-More/Mental-Health-By-the-Numbers.
2. What is Mental Health? (n.d.). Retrieved July 17, 2019, from https://www.mentalhealth.gov/basics/what-is-mental-health.
3. Mumford, G. (2016). *The Mindful Athlete: Secrets to Pure Performance*. Berkeley, CA: Parallax Press.
4. Emotional Intelligence. (n.d.). Retrieved December 30, 2019, from https://www.psychologytoday.com/us/basics/emotional-intelligence.
5. Gordon, B. (2020, February 20). Where Is My Mind?: Ben Gordon. Retrieved February 21, 2020, from https://www.theplayerstribune.com/en-us/articles/ben-gordon-mental-health-nba.
6. Take a Deep Breath. (2017, January 4). Retrieved January 12, 2020, from https://www.stress.org/take-a-deep-breath.
7. Brown, A. (2014, April 28). How Many Breaths Do You Take Each Day? Retrieved July 17, 2019, from https://blog.epa.gov/2014/04/28/how-many-breaths-do-you-take-each-day/
8. Antanaityte, N. (n.d.) Mind Matters: How To Effortlessly Have More Positive Thoughts Retrieved July 17, 2019, from https://tlexinstitute.com/how-to-effortlessly-have-more-positive-thoughts/
9. Love, K. (2018, March 6). Everyone Is Going Through Something: By Kevin Love. Retrieved February 22, 2020, from https://www.theplayerstribune.com/en-us/articles/kevin-love-everyone-is-going-through-something.

CPSIA information can be obtained
at www.ICGtesting.com
Printed in the USA
BVHW012147230822
645341BV00008B/342